ONE GOD:
PEOPLES OF THE BOOK

ONE GOD:

PEOPLES OF THE BOOK

Edited by
Edith S. Engel
and
Henry W. Engel

NEW YORK   THE PILGRIM PRESS

To Brooke and Adam
our two Jewish grandchildren

And to Kim and Stuart
our two Catholic grandchildren

with much love and gratitude
for providing our inspiration and incentive

Book design by Publishers' WorkGroup

Library of Congress Cataloging-in-Publication Data

One God : peoples of the book / edited by
Henry W. Engel and Edith S. Engel.
p.   cm.
Includes index.
ISBN 0-8298-0828-0
1. Judaism. 2. Christianity. 3. Islam. 4. Monotheism.
I. Engel, Henry W. II. Engel, Edith S.
BL80.2.O64   1990
291.1'4—dc20   90-43909
CIP

The Pilgrim Press, 475 Riverside Drive, New York, N.Y. 10115

CONTENTS

PREFACE:
WHY THIS BOOK?

This book has been a personal pilgrimage, but not to Lourdes, the Wailing Wall, Mecca, or the Holy Land. Our journey has been dictated by the need to confirm our belief that we are a family of people who can live together in peace, regardless of the differences among our liturgical languages.

But why this book? Aware that our own family now includes three of the four major monotheistic faiths in the United States, we searched for but could not find a book that would clarify what bonded our family in a religious relationship comparable to its other dimensions.

Learning about other religious traditions can open a door to an understanding of and respect for our fellow human beings, even though we celebrate our one God differently. Often we hear only about the negative, sensational, noninclusive aspects of religious beliefs and observances. As a result, many who work for peace and mutual appreciation have been frustrated by what has been presented as the inevitability of religious intolerance whose natural consequence is even, at times, a political conflict.

Undeniably, intolerance and religious conflict predate our times: Pharaoh Ramses II persecuted the Israelites at the time of Moses; the Roman emperors tortured and slaughtered the early Christians. The Crusades, the Inquisition, the sixteenth-century Wars of Religion in France and other conflicts of the Reformation period, the flights of the Pilgrims from the Netherlands and England, and that of Roger Williams from Massachusetts to Rhode Island are all examples of the historic theme of intolerance that peaked in the ultimate horror of the Holocaust.

Today there are tremendous opportunities to know about other faiths and peoples. Books, newspapers, radio, television, and magazines are readily available. Much has been written previously about Judaism, Catholicism, and Protestantism by members of those faiths; that is not so with Islam, however. For the most part a non-Muslim's knowledge of Islam comes from other non-Muslims, rather than from someone who has directly experienced the faith. As differentiated from the other monotheistic faiths, Islam is a theocracy; it embraces all aspects of existence—social, religious, and political. Media focus has been almost exclusively on the political, with the result that few non-Muslims have an accurate knowledge of the Islamic *faith*. Ignorance about religion persists; it at times seems to lead inexorably to hostility and bigotry, one faith against another. We must have an open mind to examine our respective beliefs from historic and spiritual perspectives and to know where we have come from, where we are, and where we can go with enlightenment.

This book is an effort to discuss the monotheistic religions—Judaism, Catholicism, Protestantism, and Islam—acknowledging their similarities rather than dwelling on their differences, with the hope of embracing their commonality and continuity throughout history. We intend this to be a primer that will explain each faith, show its meaning, and allow readers to explore religions with which they are less familiar. With knowledge and understanding, constructive steps toward peace in this troubled and confused world may be possible. There are, of course, other religions that aspire to peaceful coexistence; for the purposes of this book, however, we have focused on those religions that are monotheistic and have looked at them essentially from the viewpoint of the United States.

The basic discussion of each of the first three religions has been written by an authoritative voice within each faith. In the case of Islam, however, we have varied somewhat from that basic pattern: a highly accredited non-Muslim scholar has written that chapter, with the exception of a brief exposition on the misconceptions about fundamentalism by a political scientist of the Muslim faith.

As a young doctoral candidate in religion and philosophy wrote us with reference to this book: "It is scarcely possible to overemphasize the need for the great religious faiths of our era to continue to grow in their knowledge and understanding of each other, except for the fact that, sadly enough, so few religious believers understand their *own* faiths adequately. May the attempt at fostering appreciation and understanding among the monotheistic religions by your book send each reader back to his or her own tradition to find out not only what he or she is but *why.*"

Accordingly, a member of each faith follows the original discussion with a personal essay on why she or he is, chooses to be, or has become a Jew, a Catholic, a Protestant, or a Muslim. These writers speak more personally in expressing their feelings and fervor for, as well as their commitment to, their respective religions.

Yet it is important to note that it is virtually impossible for any one person to represent all the sects, denominations, or branches of a religion when writing in a personal fashion. Thus, for example, Judaism is discussed from the perspective of only one of the three major branches of that faith. Roman Catholicism, often understood to be a unified expression of faith, has within it a variety of approaches to what is most important to its followers. Protestantism is discussed by a Presbyterian, one of more than a score of distinct denominations, and the essay "Why I Am a Muslim" represents the feelings of an American-born convert to Islam. We suggest that you look upon these personal essays as a series of intimate expressions that add further dimensions to the informational chapters that immediately precede them.

We in the United States have limited power, if any, to curtail conflict in other areas of the world. But we can do something about the misconceptions and misunderstandings that exist in our own land. We have been given by our Founding Fathers a Constitution that provides, clearly and without equivocation, for the equality of all religions. None is superior; none is or can be a state religion. Discrimination on the basis of religion has been prohibited time and again by appropriate interpretation of the Constitution's First Amendment.

But, while welcome, this legal protection should not be necessary. It is our hope that with the knowledge and understanding offered by this book there will follow some tolerance, greater objectivity, and freedom from bigotry.

Finally, in the development of *One God: Peoples of the Book,* we, as individuals, as parents and grandparents, have been the objects of our own goals. In our effort and in what we, too, have learned, we trust we have become more knowledgeable, more inspired, and more tolerant.

EDITH S. ENGEL
HENRY W. ENGEL

ACKNOWLEDGMENTS

We should like to express our appreciation to the following persons for invaluable advice, suggestions, cooperation, support, and exhortation in the search for One God: Lois J. Anderson, American Bible Society; Charles Austin, former religion reporter, *The New York Times*; Professor Peter J. Awn, Columbia University; Paul Bernabeo, formerly of *The Encyclopedia of Religion*; Ellen Bettman, A World of Difference; Muhammad Zahir Bozai, Islamic Society of Westchester and Rockland; Winifred Clark, Wainwright House; Rabbi Norman M. Cohen, Congregation Bet Shalom; Thomas D. D'Andrea, Opus Dei, Notre Dame University; Robert Dilzer, social studies department, Newtown High School, Conn.; Professor Isma'il R. al Faruqi, Temple University; Monsignor Peter G. Finn, Archdiocese of New York; Joseph G. Hopkins, editorial consultant; Pastor Robert S. MacLennan, Hitchcock Presbyterian Church; Pastor Richard B. Martin, Larchmont Avenue Church; Ghassan Nakshbendi, Islamic Cultural Center of New York; Rabbi Joseph Potasnik, Congregation Mount Sinai, New York Board of Rabbis; Robert Reiser, National Writers Union; St. Clair Richard, editor and journalist; Pastor Henry Schriever, Lutheran Church of Our Redeemer; Dr. Byron E. Shafer, Fordham University; Margaret L. Shafer, National Council of Churches; Rabbi Jeffrey Sirkman, Larchmont Temple; Dr. R. Marston Speight, Hartford Seminary.

INTRODUCTION

JAMES P. CARSE

Certainly one of the most important events in the history of the world's major religions is Abraham's departure from the land of his fathers in order to worship a single deity. This event, which occurred four thousand years ago, is the earliest known effort to establish a clearly monotheistic religion.

While wandering in the land of Canaan, Abraham entered into a compact, or covenant, with God. According to the terms of this agreement Abraham would remain faithful to God, and God would reward Abraham with descendants numbering "as the stars of the heavens." Abraham did remain true to his part of the agreement, and God did reward him, but in a somewhat surprising way. Whereas God blessed Abraham with eight children, only the first two were included in God's covenant. The oldest of the children was Ishmael, the son born to Hagar, handmaiden of Abraham's wife, Sarah. The second child, Isaac, was born to Sarah when she was many years beyond the normal childbearing years.

Abraham did not live long enough to know any of his children's children. But if he could stand where we are and look back over the four-thousand-year history of his descendants, he would see that God's promise to him had been richly fulfilled. For not only Jews but also Christians and Muslims consider themselves "children of Abraham." That is, each of the major religions of the Western world—

James P. Carse, Ph.D., is Professor of Religion at New York University. He was the host for eight years of a television program, "The Way to Go." Professor Carse is the author of *The Meaning of Faith, The Silence of God,* and *Finite and Infinite Games.*

Judaism, Christianity, and Islam—understands itself to be included in that original promise.

It is true that the story of Abraham is found in the Hebrew Bible, and that Jews can be justified in assuming that God's promise to Abraham refers primarily, if not entirely, to them. But Christians, who have always regarded the Hebrew Scriptures as part of their own Bible, have therefore assumed that they too are among those descendants numbered "as the stars of the heavens." When the Christian Scriptures were written, most of their authors still considered themselves Jews and referred to Abraham as the father of faith.

The relation between Muslims and Abraham is a little more complicated. When Muhammad received the Qur'an, the Islamic Scriptures, from the angel Gabriel, he recorded the belief that Muslims are directly descended from Ishmael, the first son of Abraham. Although Muslims tell the story of Abraham in a way that closely resembles the Bible's account, there are some details that vary from the biblical account, and some that are not found in the Bible. Muslims believe, for example, that Abraham came to Mecca and established there the Ka'ba, the holy building that is now the central place of worship for all Islam.

Generally, and while there are some variations in detail, none of the three Western religions denies to the others the privilege of referring to themselves as children of Abraham. So an interesting, perhaps even disturbing, question arises: If Jews, Christians, and Muslims all believe they come from the same source, why do they remain in three separate religions? They all acknowledge the same father, but they seem to treat each other as though they were three different families.

This question is sometimes asked another way: Is there not one true religion that lies behind Judaism, Christianity, and Islam but is not identical with any of them? This question implies that each religion, as it currently exists, is partly in error.

We are presented here with a dilemma. On the one hand, there is indeed something exclusive about each of the three religions, for it is not possible to be a Jew and a Muslim, or a Muslim and a Christian. To further complicate matters, there are divisions within each religion that are often quite exclusive. For example, it is not possible for a Jew to be both Reform and Orthodox, or for a Muslim to be both Sunni and Shi'ite. Protestant and Catholic Christians are so distinct from one another that they require two separate chapters in this book. In other words, to be an authentic participant in any of the religions under study here involves choosing not to be a participant in the others. This does not have to mean that each religion must be actively opposed to the others, only that each recognizes that it is distinct from the others.

On the other hand, if we are unhappy with the exclusive character of religious faith and want to find a solid basis for unifying all traditions, we can do so only by declaring to each that it is somehow in error. We might reason that since all these religions cannot be equally true without contradicting one another, they must be equally false, and that the truth therefore lies elsewhere. This puts us in the peculiar, if not arrogant, position, for example, of attempting to explain to Muslims the true meaning of Islam, as though centuries of worship and study have only deepened their errors. Arrogant or not, this is a tempting way of approaching religion, a way that is sometimes thought to be liberal and open-minded, even reasonable.

There is another difficulty that thwarts any attempt we may make to find one "true" religion. Since all believers in the Western religions regard themselves as children of Abraham, we may conclude that it is possible to find something in the story of Abraham on which a common tradition could be built. The difficulty here is that each religion has a somewhat different understanding of Abraham's actual role in history, and the only way we can get back to Abraham is through the specific memory each religion has of him. There is no knowledge of Abraham outside the religious traditions: no archeological remains and no references to him in the literature of other cultures exist. In short, there is no possibility of knowing who Abraham the man really was. We can only have a Jewish or Islamic or Christian understanding of him.

What are we to make of all of this? Must we conclude that either one of these religions is true or they all are false? There is, happily, one other conclusion to draw, which is suggested in each of the religions itself in a powerful theme that repeatedly surfaces in all of the religious traditions under discussion here. While Jews, Muslims, Catholic Christians, and Protestant Christians all believe that their respective scriptures are a true revelation of God, they also believe in the mysteriousness of the Divine, that is, that the limitations of hu-

man intelligence and experience prevent us from completely understanding that revelation.

In the Hebrew Scriptures we find the declaration that no one can
see God and live. There seems to be such a vast difference between
our existence and God's that the only way we could fully comprehend the Divine as it is in Itself is if we cease to be as we are in
ourselves. This has an interesting consequence in Jewish tradition.
Although Jews believe God's will was fully revealed in the law as it is
found in the Torah (the first five books of the Bible), they also believe
that we do not fully understand how it applies to every aspect of our
lives. Therefore, it is necessary to interpret the law over and over
again as new situations develop in human history. This constant re-
interpretation is a process that will never end. No one can say in ad-
vance, and for all time, precisely what God intends in the changing
circumstances of human life.

If we now return to our question about the truth of each of the
traditions, we can see that although Jews can insist their religion is
an authentic response to God's revelation, there are still divine secrets
that will always elude them. Judaism as such is not false, but it does
not capture the whole truth in a final form.

We find similar themes in Islam and Christianity. The Muslims'
Qur'an often gives readers the impression that it has no structure, no
apparent organization. The suras (chapters) are arranged not by historical or thematic sequence, for example, but by their relative
lengths: the longest at the beginning, the shortest at the end. Concerning this apparent disorder there is an old Islamic teaching that
the Qur'an is quite clear and sequential, a precise disclosure of the
divine mind in all its perfect order. The disorder is not in the Qur'an
but in the readers who, because of human inadequacies, cannot see
the truth directly.

The inability of the mind to master divine mysteries does not, of
course, prevent some persons from thinking they can know the divine will—for themselves as well as for others—with complete accu-
racy. These so-called absolutists, or fundamentalists, regularly emerge
in each of the religious traditions. Their positions can be made inef-
fective through a sound knowledge of the history of religion, for each
history plainly shows how any given absolutist position soon draws
opposition to itself, often by other absolutists.

To any student of Christian history, for example, it quickly becomes obvious that there are enormous differences in the way Scripture is read and applied to everyday life; a consensus can be found only on a relatively small number of items. There are sober and intelligent readers of the Christian Scriptures who believe from their study of the Gospels that Christians should live as communists, possessing no private property whatsoever. Other Christians believe financial prosperity is a sign of God's blessing on their honest labor, and are repelled by the possibility of relinquishing private wealth. On any number of other questions—such as the number of sacraments, the ordination of women, pacifism, abortion, and homosexuality—Christians have arrived at no universal agreement. Yet many seem not to realize the impossibility of making the Bible speak unambiguously on every human conflict, and consider their individual views to be the only ones grounded in Christianity.

What I suggest is this: At their most profound levels each one of the Western religions recognizes a divine incomprehensibility so vast that no human may presume to speak for God. If there are differences between religions or between persons within the same religion, they are human differences that arise from our common ignorance. When we disagree on religious matters, we should not therefore try to prove each other wrong, but attempt instead to see that neither of us has a full grasp of the truth. In this recognition we can begin to see how we are in fact all brothers and sisters.

I cannot be both a Jew and a Muslim, but the only way I can be either a "good" Jew or a "good" Muslim is to focus on the differences between myself and God, not on the differences between myself and other persons. This leads us to a kind of paradox: those persons who have most deeply and authentically entered into their own tradition will live at peace with those of other traditions. True Christians, for instance, do not see Jews and Muslims as false, but have genuine respect for all of those who are true to their own traditions—for true Christians understand they do not fully possess the truth.

The children of Abraham have most certainly prospered. They have become a family so large that it now includes more than half of the population of the earth. There is, of course, a comparably large variety of religious styles and practices in a group so large and widely distributed. Each of the essays in this book shows most effectively how traditions develop, how the religious life is not a matter of simply having defensible beliefs or clear rules to live by. Religions are to be understood as rich human contexts, full of custom and elaborate social structures, developed over many centuries. I hope this book will be read as a celebration of the multitude of ways in which persons have responded to God. It is a book that invites its readers to a deeper appreciation of their own religious heritage by way of a fuller appreciation of the heritages of others.

1

JUDAISM

ANDREW S. ACKERMAN

According to the Hebrew Bible, the first Hebrew was Abraham. As described in the Book of Genesis, Abraham left his home in Harran in northern Mesopotamia to journey to a promised land. During his travels, Abraham moved through an ancient Near Eastern world that already had a history of more than a thousand years. From Egypt to Sumer, settled culture began with the discovery of how to cultivate food; civilization came about through the invention of writing, and progressed to the building of great cities. It was a world of polytheism, many gods, a world where the fertility goddess was adored, the rain god praised to secure crops and water, and numerous other gods solicited for their attributes—fire, thunder, wind, to name a few.

Within this context of tens of dozens of gods, tradition says the revolutionary belief in one God, the concept of monotheism, was introduced. Beginning with Abraham, monotheism slowly became the way of life of a group of people first known as Hebrews. In time they would be called Israelites (after Israel, the name given by God to Jacob, grandson of Abraham) and, finally, Jews. Our primary source for this segment of human history is the Hebrew Bible, the first five books of which are called the Torah. The Torah begins with the creation of the world and moves forward in time through the period of Abraham to the Exodus from Egypt of the Israelite tribes, ending with the set-

Andrew S. Ackerman is Director of the Arts in Education Program of the New York State Council on the Arts. He was formerly the assistant director of the Jewish Museum in New York City, where he supervised educational programs. He is co-author with Susan L. Braunstein of *Israel in Antiquity: From David to Herod*, which won the National Jewish Book Award in 1982.

tlement of the tribes in the land of Israel. Within the Torah are found the basic laws of Judaism, including the Ten Commandments. It is the single most important document for Jews around the world, for it is the core of Jewish worship and the source of much Jewish culture to this day.

From their home in the biblical land of Israel (geographically approximate to the modern state of Israel), Jews migrated throughout the world. A great, and forced, dispersion of Jews took place in 598 B.C.E., and again in 587–86 B.C.E., when Babylonian troops captured the capital city of Jerusalem and destroyed the Temple. Then, some thousand years after King David had established Israel as an independent nation, and following repeated invasions and conquests by foreign powers, the holy city of Jerusalem was destroyed by the Romans (70 C.E.). The Temple was burned and plundered, and the Jews were sent into exile, forbidden in Jerusalem. As a result, more Jews were dispersed throughout the world. Even today, those Jews living outside of Israel are said to live in the Diaspora, or Dispersion.

Small groups of Jews traveled in almost every direction. Some joined Jewish communities that had existed outside of Israel for centuries; others formed new communities. From the Middle East, Jews migrated to Europe, to other parts of Asia, and to North Africa. Later communities developed as far east as India and China. And when European civilization moved west to the Americas, Jews were part of that migration, finally reaching what is now the United States in 1654.

Who, then, is a Jew? We may think of some obvious stereotypes: the man with a long beard, dressed in a knee-length black coat and black hat; the man wearing a yarmulke, small skullcap, on his head; a person with a hooked nose and obviously Semitic features. But such stereotypes are easily shattered by a black-skinned Jew from Africa or a Jew from Scotland wearing a kilt. In fact, a Jew may speak any one of dozens of languages, may have hair color ranging from red to blond to black, and may have grown up in a country on any of five of the six continents. What binds all of these diverse people together? Physical appearance and geographical location aside, what makes being a Jew something that can be shared with another Jew no matter what his or her background?

The answer may be found in the heritage shared by all Jews. With each migration, with each new country, Jews carried with them their own culture and values, observing the same Sabbath Day and the same important days of the Jewish calendar. Flowing from the Bible and deeply embedded in holidays and celebrations, Jewish tradition also emphasizes how people should treat one another and care for the less fortunate.

WHAT DOES IT MEAN TO BE JEWISH?

If you were to ask a dozen different Jews in America, "Why do you consider yourself to be a Jew?" you would receive a dozen very different answers. Because of the long, diverse history of the Jews, there are innumerable ways in which an individual might identify him- or herself as a Jew. For a great many their identity is deeply rooted in religion and in religious practice. Others, however, connect their "Jewishness" to a cultural heritage: their "culture" is their connection to an identity based on shared experiences with others. Many people identify themselves as Jews because they consider their values to be "Jewish," even if they themselves do not follow Jewish ritual. Additionally, traditions such as caring for the underprivileged; a shared language such as Yiddish, Hebrew, or Ladino; or sensibility to a "Jewish sense of humor" are all cited as reasons for identifying oneself as a Jew. By Jewish religious law, however, a person can be accepted as a Jew only if born to a Jewish mother or converted by appropriate religious ritual.

Even among practicing Jews, that is, those Jews who belong to a synagogue and observe religious rituals at home, there is a wide range of beliefs. Jews, like members of other faiths, decide how closely they will adhere to traditional beliefs. All religions are composed of a set of beliefs that usually carry with them rituals or required behaviors. An observant Catholic attends church every Sunday and, for example, will follow the teachings of the church with regard to marriage and divorce. Jewish religious practice is a compilation of the Written Law found in the Torah, which Jews believe was given by God to Moses on Mount Sinai, and the so-called Oral Law, which is found in the Talmud. The Talmud represents centuries of interpretation of the Hebrew Bible by rabbis considered to be authorities. The Talmud is essentially composed of two parts, the Mishnah, a collection of legal interpretations and a codification of traditional practices, and the Gemara, a further commentary on the Mishnah. These provide legal and theological guidelines for Jewish life.

Throughout the ages, Jews have studied the Torah and the Talmud, argued the merits of individual interpretations, and sought to apply their laws and theology to an ever-changing world. From ancient times, there have been Jews who have followed the law to the letter. Others, however, have elected to modify the law in response to the needs of their own world. We find such differences evident in the writing of Jews from as far back as nineteen hundred years ago, when the Jewish religion underwent a dramatic change.

For a thousand years, from the time of King Solomon until the destruction of the Second Temple in 70 c.e., the center of Judaism was the Jerusalem Temple, and, tradition tells us, local religious centers were frowned upon. When the Babylonians destroyed the first Temple (587–86 b.c.e.), the priestly practice of ritual animal sacrifices on behalf of the people was disrupted for about seventy years. But Jews returned to Israel and rebuilt the Temple (hence the name Second Temple) and continued the animal sacrifices. The sacrifices, generally of a bull, lamb, goat, or bird, were in gratitude for God's bounty, cleansing of sin, and expiation.

The destruction of the Second Temple by the Romans shattered biblical Judaism in many ways. The Temple was burned, and the practice of sacrifice went up in flames with the magnificent structure. Jews were dispersed around the world, and the revered priesthood no longer had a function. By all expectations, Judaism would have ceased to exist, as had many other ancient religions. But the power of the Torah was such that the religion was able to survive a unique transformation. Local meeting places, known as synagogues, became more commonplace and Jews met to study and pray. There emerged a new position of leadership, the rabbi, who became both the social and religious fulcrum of the community. Prayer, which had always been a part of Jewish tradition, became the center of worship. A new form of Judaism was created, one that was both a continuation of biblical Judaism and also a departure from some of the ancient rituals. It has been almost two thousand years since that change took place.

Since the early nineteenth century a variety of religious options for Jews has emerged. Today there are three major branches of Judaism:

Orthodox, Reform, and Conservative. Each branch maintains the belief in the primacy of the Torah and the Talmud, with the synagogue and the rabbi as central institutions. They differ in how strictly traditional laws (the *halaka*) are observed. Orthodox Jews must observe biblical and Talmudic laws most closely, structuring their lives so that daily prayer, dietary laws, holidays, and the Sabbath can be observed. The most tenacious adherents to the ancient law and tradition are the *Hasidim,* or pious ones. The Hasidic movement, begun in Eastern Europe during the eighteenth century, follows the teaching of the charismatic Israel Baal Shem Tov. Hasidic life is religious life, with the joy of study and worship infiltrating all levels of existence. It is characterized by ecstatic worship and is known the world over for the traditional male dress of long black coats and broad-brimmed black hats. There are many different Hasidic sects, each with its own leader and with varying interpretations of how Hasidic life should be conducted. The two centers of Hasidim are in the United States and Israel.

The concept of denominations within Judaism is relatively recent. Until the Emancipation in Western Europe, in the first part of the nineteenth century, there was little deviation from traditional practice among all Jewish communities. That situation began to change, however, soon after Jews were granted rights of citizenship and allowed entry into European society. Jews began to consider ways in which traditional practice might be modified. The early reformers offered sermons in the vernacular, which in most cases was German; they introduced an organ and choir into the liturgy, and they allowed women and men to sit together during the service. While seemingly cosmetic, these early changes were actually quite profound, for such modifications encouraged the retention of Jewish tradition while allowing for the influence of European mores.

The initial changes gave way to a more comprehensive system of reforming Judaism. Reform Jews encourage the use of scientific analysis of the Hebrew Bible and other Jewish texts and have supported the notion of informed choice, a legacy which exists to this day. As a result, we may say that Reform Judaism sees itself as a movement of choice, with individuals choosing those aspects of traditional belief that make sense in their lives. The world has changed a great deal since biblical times, and Reform Jews seek to mold a life that takes into account the modern twentieth-century world. Although Reform

Judaism began in Germany in the early nineteenth century, it flourished earliest in the United States, particularly among the German Jews who settled there.

Conservative Judaism also began in Europe, and its hallmark was the importance of historical continuity. For Conservative Jews the changes beginning even two hundred years ago were not enough cause to abandon the tradition and practices which have sustained the Jewish community for thousands of years. Consequently, Conservative Jews are more careful to maintain aspects of the traditional life that are considered to be intrinsic. These include observance of the Sabbath, the holidays, and the dietary laws.

(A fourth branch of Judaism, the Reconstructionists, is a recent twentieth-century movement. More a culture than a theology, it recognizes aspects of the other three major branches.)

Within the three major branches of Judaism there are differences from individual to individual and from synagogue to synagogue. Recently, some families have begun to form their own study and worship groups, not affiliated with any formal Jewish denomination or ethnic body. Each such group is called a *havurah,* or friends group.

CULTURAL DIVERSITY IN THE
JEWISH COMMUNITY

It is difficult to define in cultural terms what being Jewish means. It is a fact that many Jews identify themselves as Jews although they are not affiliated with a synagogue and do not practice the religion, because so much of Jewish culture stems from the Torah or Talmud. Judaism is definitely a religion but it is not one culture, for Jews live the world over and have absorbed an extraordinary range of cultural traits from other peoples. Jews are generally divided into three ethnic groups, although some, such as the Ethiopian Jews, or Falashas, fall outside these boundaries: (1) Ashkenazim, or European Jews; (2) Oriental, or Middle Eastern Jews; (3) Sephardim, the Jews expelled from the Iberian peninsula in 1492.

The story of the Oriental Jews begins in the biblical period when Jews lived in cities throughout the ancient Near East (the modern Middle East). Prior to the destruction of the Temple in Jerusalem by the Babylonians in 586 B.C.E., there is little knowledge of any community outside of Israel. With the exile of the Jews to Babylon, a large community was established in Mesopotamia. Later communities developed in Alexandria, Egypt, Turkey, Syria, and Persia, peopled by Jews thoroughly Middle Eastern in culture, language, food, dress, and the architecture of their synagogues. Some communities, such as those in Baghdad and Cairo, two of the most ancient Jewish communities outside of Israel, trace their roots to biblical times.

The story of the Ashkenazic and the Sephardic Jews is generally the story of the Diaspora. Sephardic Jews take their name from the Hebrew word for Spain, *Sepharad*. The Jewish community in Spain is an ancient one, beginning perhaps as early as before the destruction of the Second Temple. At first the community was small and spread throughout small villages and towns. Earliest records date from the fourth century, when regulations controlling relations between Christians and Jews were written down. Two centuries later, when Christianity became the state religion, the first laws limiting Jewish rights were instituted. The resulting persecution led to an exodus of Jews from Spain to North Africa and a period of oppression that did not end until the conquest of Spain by the Arabs in the year 711.

By the tenth century, under Islamic rule in Spain, Jews began to develop a growing intellectual and cultural community. Beginning in the eleventh century, and reaching a zenith in the twelfth and thirteenth centuries, Spanish cities such as Toledo became centers of European culture; Jewish scholarship, philosophy, and literature flourished. Traditional Jewish culture absorbed features of both Spanish and Islamic culture, as evidenced by the art and architecture of Jewish manuscripts and synagogues of the period.

However, toward the end of the fourteenth century, prosperity and relative freedom began to end for the Jews as Spanish Christians regained control of their country. Persecution by Christians resulted in the deaths of thousands of Jews; those who saw no other way to save their lives converted. For decades, the problem of what to do with the Jews who would not convert continued. One proposal, put forth in the 1300s, was to expel Jews from Spain, not an original idea, for Jews had been expelled from England in 1290 and from France in 1306 because of anti-Semitism.

In 1492 the Jews were expelled from Spain by Ferdinand and Isabella. From Spain, some fled to Portugal (from which they were later also expelled), others to North Africa, Turkey, and the Middle East. They resettled in these countries and merged their Spanish/Jewish culture with local customs. In some places, such as Turkey, although the Sephardic Jews maintained their language (Ladino, a mixture of Hebrew and Spanish), they coexisted with other Jewish groups. While the Sephardim have also, in the course of time, migrated to other parts of the world—Europe and the United States, for instance—those who remained in the Middle East are considered the predominant Jewish group there. The earlier Oriental Jews are now considered among the Sephardim.

The Jews of Central and Eastern Europe are known as Ashkenazic Jews. During the Roman Empire, Jews lived in Italy, France, and, to a lesser extent, Germany. Their settlements remained small, with the majority of world Jewry still in the Middle East. The Jews were seldom permitted the stability that would allow them to put down roots, nor were they permitted to own land; they were traders and businesspeople. As European communities began to grow in the twelfth and thirteenth centuries, slowly extending eastward toward Poland, Jews followed.

Facilitating the spread of Jews throughout Europe was a common language that gradually came into being at this time: Yiddish. It contained elements of various European tongues—Italian, French, German—together with words and phrases from the ancient Hebrew languages, and over time picked up additional words from other national languages. Yiddish spread as Jews moved across Europe to the east, becoming the common cultural tongue that has bound Jews together to this day wherever they may be in the world. Yiddish has no alphabet of its own; it uses the alphabet of Hebrew and follows the Hebrew practice of writing from right to left. Hebrew has generally retained a separate identity as the language of the religion and its liturgy.

Throughout the Middle Ages the Jews were alternately persecuted and allowed to enjoy relative freedom. They were frequently segregated from Christian society. In Eastern Europe they lived in small villages known as *shtetls;* within the shtetls there developed a rich culture known as *Yiddishkeit.* Jewish intellectual life also flourished in the cities, especially after the turn of the nineteenth century when in Western Europe Jews were granted equal rights under the law. The extension of legal rights was in response to the example of the United

States Constitution, picked up first by France following its own revolution. Emancipation allowed Jews to choose from a greater variety of life styles than had ever been available. They became involved in the arts and sciences, eventually producing such important authors as Franz Kafka and scientists such as Sigmund Freud and Albert Einstein.

At the turn of the nineteenth century most of the world's Jewry lived in Europe, particularly in the Pale of Settlement. The Pale, today part of Poland and Russia, was a region within which Jews were forced to live to prevent their spreading to other areas of czarist Russia. It was also the site, beginning in the 1880s, of great pogroms (massacres of Jews). While these pogroms were horrible, they were but a foreshadowing of the horror of the Holocaust that was to confront the Jews of Europe during World War II.

"A LIFE OF TORAH, WORSHIP, AND GOOD DEEDS"

Among the sayings collected in the Mishnah, which, together with the Gemara makes up the Talmud, is a summary of a Jew's obligations, written by High Priest Simeon the Just, a third-century B.C.E. scholar. He wrote that a Jew should be raised to live a life of Torah, worship, and good deeds, the three elements that form the crux of what being a Jew has encompassed over the centuries. This tradition has become even more than a religious focal point; it has become the center of Jewish culture. A life of Torah and worship is a life of study, and nothing is more valued than learning in most traditional Jewish homes. In addition, the Bible and Talmud are very clear in instructing Jews to care for the disadvantaged or persecuted. Such teaching has led to an extraordinary level of Jewish involvement in charity work and active participation in such causes as the civil rights movement in the United States.

These values are upheld in the home and the synagogue. Many Jewish holidays and celebrations have rituals that retell historical events to remind Jews of their past and their obligation to the present. Through celebration a Jew relives past experiences and passes on from generation to generation both tradition and values.

HOMELIFE, THE COMMUNITY, AND
THE SYNAGOGUE

Homelife

It is difficult to separate completely the home and the synagogue when one discusses Jewish ritual and practice. Many of the religious practices that are part of family life are also integral to the synagogue service. For example, observance of the Sabbath begins in the home on Friday night and is often continued with prayer in the synagogue on Saturday morning. The family, through the celebration of holidays and special events that mark important moments in a person's life, is the mainstay in the perpetuation of Jewish tradition.

Judaism sanctifies time and everyday life. This means that during every moment of a person's life he or she should try to emulate God. To help people to accomplish this, Judaism has organized a person's daily routine according to cycles of time. The cycle with the largest scope is that of historical time. The Torah reminds us constantly of historical events that took place during the time of the Hebrew Bible and urges Jews to remember such crucial historical events as the Exodus of the Jewish people from Egypt. Recalling this event not only reminds Jews of their rescue from slavery by God, celebrated by the Passover, but also relates Jews of later time periods to their past.

Traditional Jewish life also sanctifies a person's life by prescribing daily, weekly, and annual prayer and holidays. Four cycles are central to the practice of Judaism:

1. Daily prayer, three times a day (see "Community and Synagogue," p. 20);
2. A day of rest, the Sabbath, from Friday evening to Saturday evening;
3. An annual cycle of holidays;
4. The life cycle of an individual that marks birth, puberty, marriage, and death with religious ceremonies.

The Sabbath.   The idea of a day of rest during the week is one of Judaism's major contributions to Western civilization. The Sabbath is the period from twilight on Friday to sundown on Saturday. During this period, one is to rest from all physical labor, recalling the fact that God rested on the seventh day after the creation of the world.

In a traditional Jewish home, the Sabbath officially begins with the lighting of Sabbath candles on Friday evening. According to tradition, the lights are kindled by the mother or an older daughter. In most European Jewish traditions candlesticks are used; in Oriental and Sephardic traditions oil lamps are used. The Sabbath lights separate the regular workweek from the Holy Sabbath. Saturday morning is marked by prayer at the synagogue, and the afternoon is taken up with family-oriented activities.

The end of the Sabbath is also marked by the lighting of candles. The *Havdalah* ceremony is one of the favorite times of the week for families: a specially braided candle is lighted and sweet spices are passed around the table so that all will remember the sweetness of the Sabbath and look forward to the next one. Havdalah (literally, "separation") is a momentary pause before the workweek begins, a moment to reflect upon the prayers and thoughts of the Sabbath.

Holidays.   The annual cycle of holidays begins with the Jewish New Year, Rosh Hashanah. This early fall holiday occurs in September or October: its exact date each year is determined by the Jewish lunar calendar. Nine days after Rosh Hashanah is the holiest day of the Jewish year, Yom Kippur. On this Day of Atonement Jews are to reflect upon the year just completed, to be penitent, and to solemnly vow better conduct in the coming year. It is a day of fasting and prayer. Rosh Hashanah and Yom Kippur are called the High Holy Days; the time between the two holidays is called the Days of Awe.

Two additional fall holidays are Sukkot and Simchat Torah. Sukkot is an eight-day holiday celebrating the autumn harvest in Israel. It is, together with Passover and Shauvot, one of the three most ancient holidays, those that existed when Jews journeyed to the Temple in Jerusalem to offer a sacrifice. That practice came to an end when the Temple was destroyed in 70 C.E. Sukkot also recalls the wandering of the Israelites in the desert after the Exodus from Egypt. To commemorate that event, Jews erect wooden huts or booths to simulate the booths that the Israelites may have constructed in the desert. Simchat Torah is a one-day celebration that occurs at the end of Sukkot. This holiday celebrates the end of the yearly cycle of the reading of the Torah in the synagogue.

The only traditional winter festival in Judaism is Hanukkah. It is both a religious holiday and a celebration of freedom, based on the achievement of Jewish independence from the Greek-Syrians in the year 164 B.C.E. Its religious significance comes from the legend that the victorious solidiers, in entering the Temple for a celebration, found only a single day's supply of oil for the lamps. Miraculously, the oil lasted for eight days. The celebration of Hanukkah has become more elaborate in America than in any other country, including Israel. Hanukkah, like many Jewish holidays, is very child-oriented, and, since it occurs close to Christmas, it is often treated as its Jewish equivalent. The lighting of the *menorah,* the Hanukkah lamp, on each of the eight days of the holiday is a practice that children look forward to—along with the *dreidel* (a four-sided top) game and the latkes, the potato pancakes, that are served. The wide range of styles of Hanukkah lamps from around the world are symbolic of the diversity of Jewish communities and the varied artistic influences that have been absorbed by Jews over the centuries.

A modern winter holiday, occurring in mid to late January in Israel, is the New Year of the Trees *(Tu B'Shvat),* which is a ceremony of tree planting, part of the agricultural cycle, and serves the purpose of reforestation and reclamation of eroded and desert soils.

Springtime begins with Purim, a holiday that also celebrates freedom. Every year the scroll of Esther *(megillah)* is read to remember the biblical story of the triumph over Haman, a Persian official who sought to exterminate all the Jews of the Persian Empire in the fifth century B.C.E. Purim is followed by Passover, a week-long holiday that marks the Exodus of the Jews from Egypt. On the first two nights of the holiday, Jews participate in a special meal called the *seder.* During the seder, the story of the Exodus is recounted by reading the *haggadah.* The Passover holiday is also geared to children, with the youngest child in the family responsible for preparing the reading of the "four questions." These questions, and their answers, emphasize the importance of the Exodus in Jewish history and values. This seminal event in Judaism is a symbol of God's covenant with the Jews and a connection to the past for all Jews.

The third of the ancient pilgrimage holidays is Shavuot, a late spring event that celebrates the giving of the Torah to Moses by God on Mount Sinai.

With the exception of Hanukkah, Simchat Torah, and Tu B'Shvat, the Jewish holidays originated during biblical times. Each holiday is tied to a historical event and its observance is an important means of teaching the young about Jewish history and ritual. Since the date of the holiday is determined according to the Jewish calendar, Jews all over the world celebrate the holidays simultaneously. Some holidays are also tied to the ancient Israelite agricultural calendar and are associated with harvests or planting. In some places, the observance of such agricultural holidays according to the seasons in Israel is almost opposite to the local calendar. Yet the maintenance of traditional times of year has been critical in helping the Jews to maintain a group identity. Despite the fact that Passover in Moscow might be accompanied by a snowstorm while an Israeli perspires in the heat, both communities are tied together by the celebration of the holiday and the remembrance of the Exodus.

Life-Cycle Celebrations. Almost all cultures mark certain critical moments with rituals or celebrations. For Jews, birth, puberty, marriage, and death are the four moments in an individual's life that are so marked. In a similar way, life-cycle events are also a part of homelife: it is the responsibility of the family to organize the celebration in the home and to educate the children.

On the eighth day after a Jewish male child is born he is circumcised. Circumcision is a literal sign of the covenant between God and the Jewish people. According to the Hebrew Bible the covenant (*brith* in Hebrew) is the agreement that God first made with Abraham that bound Jews to pledge observance of God's law, especially the strict belief in monotheism. The circumcision ceremony is, therefore, both an individual family's celebration of a birth and the community's celebration of the addition of a new member into the covenant with God. Baby girls are brought to the synagogue for a naming ceremony that introduces them into the community. Circumcision is a particularly Jewish ceremony, later taken up by the Muslims, but as a hygienic measure, it has been adopted by many people of other faiths.

An important event in the life of a Jewish child is that time when the child is on the verge of adulthood. At the age of thirteen a boy is initiated into manhood by the ceremony called *bar mitzvah*, literally becoming a "son of the commandment." The bar mitzvah ceremony publicly acknowledges that the young man must now undertake the responsibility of keeping the commandments as would any adult in the community. Recently, girls have also begun to mark their transition into adulthood with the parallel ceremony known as *bat mitzvah*, "daughter of the commandment." The bat mitzvah was not practiced until the twentieth century and is still limited to Reform and Conservative Jews.

When a Jew decides to marry, the marriage ceremony, conducted by a rabbi, is both a civil and a religious service. The marriage calls upon the bride and groom to observe the laws of the Torah and to raise their children in the Jewish tradition.

In many Jewish communities, communal societies exist to assist families during illness or at the death of a family member. One is the burial society, which helps to prepare the dead for burial, locate a burial place, and provide support for the family during the days of mourning that follow the burial.

Traditional Judaism, as set forth in the Talmud and interpreted by the rabbis over the centuries, includes instructions for almost all aspects of everyday life. For example, dietary laws, such as the prohibition against eating pork and shellfish, introduce religious practices into every meal. Careful observance of Jewish law also requires prayer three times a day. This provides a religious context for a person's everyday labor. Even sexual relationships between husband and wife are governed by laws concerning when intercourse is permitted during the menstrual cycle. Each individual Jew decides to what extent he or she will practice traditional Judaism. Many decide to follow each of the rites to the letter. Others follow only some of the ancient traditions.

The Community and the Synagogue

The three principles upon which Jewish practice is based—Torah, worship, and good deeds—are applied to both the individual and the community. While Judaism stresses the responsibility of the individual, it also mandates that the individual be involved with the community at large through communal activities. Thus, the life-cycle events described above are generally conducted as community cele-

brations. Prayers, too, are offered primarily as a community observance and require ten men (*minyan*) in order for the complete worship service to take place.

The center of Jewish community life is the synagogue, which
comes from a Greek word meaning "meeting place." The genesis of
the synagogue is unknown. Tradition cites its existence as long ago as
the Babylonian exile (586–539 B.C.E.). The oldest written references
to synagogues date to before the destruction of the Second Temple
(70 C.E.). Archeological excavations have uncovered only a few synagogues that predate the Roman destruction of the Temple. In all like-
lihood, the synagogue became the preeminent Jewish institution as a
result of the loss of the Temple. Prayer, which had always been an
important part of Judaism, became formalized under the leadership
of the cantor and the rabbi in the synagogue.

The major component of the synagogue service is the reading of
the Torah. Every Sabbath, a portion of the Torah is read, with a section of the weekly reading repeated on Mondays and Thursdays. This
remains constant in synagogues throughout the world. Differences
exist in the pronunciation of the Hebrew, the melodies used to chant
the Torah, and where the Torah is housed within the synagogue. For
Jews, worship and education cannot be separated and the weekly
readings are an important religious and educational vehicle for both
children and adults. They culminate, as stated earlier, in Simchat Torah, the holiday celebrating the end of the yearly cycle of the reading
of the Torah.

Housed within the synagogue are many Jewish ceremonial objects.
The Torah, which is the central object, must be a handwritten scroll
without adornment on the parchment. The objects used to protect
and decorate the Torah, however, can take as many forms as the
imagination and funds allow. Magnificent wooden arks, some carved
with intricate patterns, hold the scrolls when they are not in use.
Some communities place their scrolls in wooden or metal cases before
returning them inside the ark. Crowns, shields, and embroidered Torah mantles all serve to beautify the Torah.

During the service the Torah is placed on a reader's desk and individuals from the congregation are called upon to read the weekly
portion. In Orthodox synagogues, any male may be asked to read; in
Reform and some Conservative synagogues, women may now be

called to read from the Torah. Men wear a traditional prayer shawl, or *tallit*, during the morning service and during holiday services. In all Orthodox and in some Conservative synagogues, men and women sit apart in different sections of the synagogue.

To someone who has never witnessed a synagogue service, some services might seem chaotic. Certain sections of the service are silent readings, and people may rise or sit as they finish prayers. Each congregant may chant the service with a different melody and at a different pace—only to be followed by the communal singing of a hymn in an accepted melody. This mixing of different traditions of a common heritage is indicative of the long, diverse history of Judaism. Some services, however, are more formal and easier to understand.

In addition to the formal service of prayers, Torah readings, and blessings, the rabbis will usually deliver a sermon on Saturday. Community announcements are delivered from the pulpit. Synagogues also house schools for children, which may vary from supplemental schools in the afternoon to full-time day schools where children learn both secular and religious subjects. It is here, too, that Conservative and Reform groups often hold confirmation classes, in which girls and boys go through a course of religious study as prescribed by their rabbis. Confirmation usually occurs at the age of fifteen or sixteen. Most synagogues include space for social activities or are associated with other community centers that may include recreational facilities.

Synagogues also spearhead and direct their congregants' charitable activities, a mainstay of Jewish tradition. Charity frequently reaches out beyond the community, serving whoever is in need. Traditional areas of Jewish concern are health, education, civil rights, and social welfare.

JEWS IN TODAY'S WORLD

Three events in the twentieth century have been crucial in Jewish history: immigration to America, the Holocaust, and the emergence of the independent state of Israel. Just as such events as the Exodus must be understood to comprehend ancient Jewish life, these three events are the keystones to understanding today's Jewish communities.

Although Jews came to America as early as 1654, it was not until the nineteenth century that their numbers began to increase dramatically. Following a wave of immigration from Western Europe in the middle of that century a flood of immigrants poured in from Eastern Europe. Beginning in the late 1800s, poverty and the pogroms of Eastern Europe forced Jews to flee their homes. Millions found refuge in America. The United States offered Jews more freedom than they had ever before encountered in the Diaspora. To be sure, they still were victims of anti-Semitism and were excluded from many levels of society, but they were equal under the law and protected from the pogroms that plagued Europe for centuries.

During the 1920s and 1930s as the Jewish community prospered in America, the situation in Europe worsened. With the German economy in ruin, Adolf Hitler rose to power. His Nazi party philosophy singled out the Jews as the cause of the ills that plagued Germany; racism became a rallying point. Hitler's war against the Jews carried with it a "final solution": the extermination of European Jewry. That final solution was put into practice in a system of concentration and death camps erected throughout Western and Eastern Europe. Jews by the thousands were rounded up and sent to camps such as Auschwitz, Dachau, and Bergen-Belsen. They were forced to live in inhuman conditions or sent to their deaths before firing squads, in gas chambers, or in ovens. By the time the Allied armies liberated the camps, more than six million European Jews had been murdered. The Holocaust, as it has come to be called, shocked the world when the facts became public. Photographs and motion pictures taken in the camps document the horror; Nazi records, carefully registering the names and occupations of inmates entering the camps, still exist.

The Holocaust has had a great impact on Jews around the world. The scars of the war years remain with many Jews who suffered losses of family members and property. Many have had to try to reconstruct their lives in new countries. Children of survivors have inherited a difficult legacy and have had to come to terms with the horror of the past in their present lives. In addition, many noble non-Jews who rescued and sheltered victims throughout the Holocaust have since borne scars and have never been the same.

Following World War II, a large number of Jews arrived in Palestine, seeking to renew roots in their ancient homeland. Many were turned away by the occupying British government, yet thousands settled and joined the already existing Jewish cities and villages. In 1948

Great Britain withdrew from Palestine and the state of Israel was born. Two thousand years had elapsed since the last independent Jewish nation had existed.

For centuries Jews had recited the words, "Next year in Jerusalem" at the end of the Passover seder. The establishment of Israel made this hope a reality. Although most Jews in the Diaspora have elected not to move to Israel, the country's existence has played an important role in the identity of world Jewry. As the twentieth century draws to a close, Judaism continues both to change and to remain the same. The experiences in America and Israel have resulted in the formation of modern Jewish communities side by side with the older, traditional ones. As they have for centuries, Jews continue to study and question their written tradition and to seek new interpretations for old and contemporary problems. And Jewish parents continue to raise their children to a life of Torah, worship, and good deeds.

2

WHY I CHOOSE JUDAISM

DEBORAH E. ZECHER

The sound of the shofar blast signaling the end of Yom Kippur . . . the smell of latkes frying on Hanukkah . . . the laughter of fifteen three- and four-year-old children decorating a sukkah with fruits and veg- etables . . . the taste of the first matzoh at the seder on Passover . . . the sight of students engrossed in the study of Jewish texts—these are among the images and sensations that draw me, both as a rabbi and as a member of the Jewish people, close to my Judaism.

If I pause to consider the components of what it means to be a Jew, I find three of utmost importance: covenant, community, and celebra- tion. I identify myself as a Jew not only because my parents are Jew- ish but even more so because I choose consciously to be part of a community bound by a four-thousand-year-old covenant with God. I define the path of my life by seasonal and lifetime Jewish celebra- tions. In a world that increasingly values secular principles, I look to my Jewish heritage for my ethics and ideals. And yet, as a liberal Jew, I live in the secular world, and so my energy is also directed toward finding a pleasing balance of the two.

As a rabbi, or "teacher," I define my task as sharing Jewish tradi- tion and history, and Jewish possibilities, with my community. The subject matter available is exciting and compelling for both children

Deborah E. Zecher is Interim Rabbi, Temple Micah, in Washington, D.C., and is also a facilitator in the U.S. Navy's professional development course for chaplains. Rabbi Zecher was for seven years the Associate Rabbi and Educational Director of the West- chester Reform Temple in Scarsdale, N.Y. She also has served as the president of the Scarsdale-Hartsdale Interfaith Clergy Organization, as well as the coordinator of the Women's Rabbinic Network.

and adults. At its best, Jewish life is the quintessential lesson plan, full of questions and some answers, replete with examples that engage every sense. As a Reform rabbi, I present the full range of Jewish choices possible to my community. Informed choice becomes the crucial phrase for liberal Judaism. Moreover, the spiritual life of a Jew is not confined to an ephemeral "other world"; rather, we experience God in the here and now. As a rabbi, I seek the opportunity to share that knowledge with my congregation.

CELEBRATION

The initial opportunity to share the fullness of Jewish life often comes through life-cycle ceremonies and the festivals of the Jewish year. We are drawn to observance of the Jewish holidays with their special worship services, rituals, foods, and music, with their moments for quiet personal introspection and exuberant communal celebration. As I think over the years of my life, I realize how closely tied my life is to the flow of the Jewish calendar. I begin my year in the autumn with the Yamim Noraim, the Days of Awe (also known as the High Holy Days), which conclude the old year and celebrate the new one. Even as my community anticipates the events of the year to come, we make an account of our actions in the year now ending. The Yamim Noraim start with Rosh Hashanah (New Year) and conclude ten days later with the fast of Yom Kippur (Day of Atonement). This is our time for evaluating all the relationships in our lives, including our bond with God, and atoning for the mistakes we have made, any hostility we may have engendered. Our tradition teaches that we cannot ask for forgiveness from God until we have been forgiven by our friends and family. It is an exciting and sobering time of the year, for when we really enter into the spirit of the holiday, we find ourselves with the opportunity to consider the relationships that make up our lives. It is a special gift to be reminded of the precious bonds that exist among people and to renew those bonds yearly.

The High Holy Days are followed by the week-long harvest festival of Sukkot, the first of the Pilgrim Festivals, so called because people would come to the Temple in Jerusalem at these times in the year. For Sukkot we construct sukkahs (flimsy huts) to commemorate the temporary shelter used by the Israelites who wandered in the desert for forty years on their way to the Promised Land. We decorate these sukkahs with the fruits and vegetables that remind us of the wonderful bounty of the harvest. Many families construct sturdier sukkahs and try to spend as much time as possible in them, eating and entertaining there throughout the holiday. We also bring cans of food to our synagogue, to be distributed to the hungry and homeless, for we are reminded that we were once homeless.

The final day of Sukkot is celebrated as Simchat Torah (Rejoicing in the Torah). We read from the Torah in weekly portions throughout the year; on Simchat Torah we finish the year's reading with the last few verses of Deuteronomy and immediately begin again with the creation of the world in Genesis. There is singing and dancing and parading through the temple with the Torah scrolls. Simchat Torah is a wonderful, joyous holiday. In most Reform congregations, Simchat Torah is also the occasion for welcoming new students to Jewish education with the ceremony of Consecration. There is nothing more beautiful than watching all the little children come up to the bema (platform where services are held) and receive a blessing of welcome. Consecration becomes an important moment of affirmation of Jewish survival.

Another holiday that affirms Jewish survival is Hanukkah, the eight-day winter festival of lights. This holiday commemorates the victory of the small Jewish army over the massive Greek-Syrian forces during the second century B.C.E. "Not by might and not by power but by My spirit alone, says God" to the people, and that becomes the message of Hanukkah. More than celebrating a military victory, we rejoice in the triumph of faith in and dedication to God over military power.

The legend of a miracle also accompanies the celebration of Hanukkah. When the Hasmoneans, the family that led the victorious Jewish army, entered the Holy Temple, they found only enough oil for the Eternal Light to last one day. Amazingly, the oil lasted eight days, enough time to seek additional supplies. As a result, Hanukkah lasts eight days. Each evening we light candles in a special candelabra called a hanukkiyah or menorah. We begin on the first night with one candle and add another every night until there are eight candles blazing on the final night of the festival. To remember the miraculous oil, we eat fried foods, especially latkes (potato pancakes). And we play with a dreidel, a specially constructed top with Hebrew letters on each side that stand for "a great miracle happened there." Hanukkah is a wonderful family-centered holiday that teaches us our history and renews our faith.

As we become more and more associated with the land of Israel, the holiday of Tu B'Shvat takes on greater importance for us. Tu B'Shvat, the Hebrew abbreviation for the fifteenth day of the Hebrew month of Shvat, is the New Year of the Trees. This is another holiday that stresses the historical connection of the Jewish people to the land. We observe this day primarily by planting or buying trees to be planted in the land of Israel. Given the despoliation of the land over the centuries, this act of purchasing trees for Israel takes on greater significance. Some Jews celebrate Tu B'Shvat by sharing in a special seder that highlights the fruits and vegetables unique to Israel. In this seder we acknowledge the gradual change of the seasons from the cold desolation of winter to the life-affirming warmth of spring.

With the advent of spring comes Purim, probably our most impulsive holiday. Purim celebrates the survival of the Jews of Persia from the evil decree of the prime minister Haman who had condemned them to death. Mordechai and Esther are the heroes of the story and we acclaim them as we read Megillat Esther (the scroll of Esther) each year. As the story is told, we stamp our feet or shout or use graggers (noisemakers) to drown out the name of Haman. Many people, especially the children, dress in costume on Purim, appearing as Mordechai or Esther or even Haman. Some communities even have Purim parades. We eat delicious three-cornered filled pastries called hamantaschen (Haman's pockets), and many people follow the custom of Shalach manot, that is, they deliver packages of food to friends and relatives. We tend to think of Purim as a children's holiday, but it really belongs to all of us because of the joy and spirit it provides for people of all ages.

One of the most familiar festivals is Pesach (Passover), the second of the Pilgrim Festivals. This seven-day holiday (eight days for traditional Jews) commemorates the Exodus of the Israelites from slavery in Egypt. It is observed both in the synagogue and at home. Families come together in their homes to share the seder, the ritual meal that begins the holiday. We use a haggadah, a kind of prayer book or order of events that tells the story of the Exodus, using as our mandate the verse: "In every generation, it is incumbent upon us to think of ourselves as though we, too, had gone out from Egypt.'' We tell this story over and over again because it is our personal story; even though we may not actually have stood at the shores of the Red Sea or at the foot of Mount Sinai, we are commanded to relive the experience as though we were there. The telling of the Exodus creates a powerful chain that spans and connects the generations.

Pesach abounds with ritual symbols. At the seder a basin, a pitcher of water, and a towel are twice passed around the table for a ceremonial washing of hands as a ritual of purification. Many symbolic items are set upon the table on a special plate. We eat bitter herbs to remind us of the horror of slavery, we dip green vegetables such as parsley in salt water to recall the tears of slavery, and we eat haroset (a mixture of chopped nuts, apples, cinnamon, and a few drops of wine), which looks like the mortar used by our ancestors between the bricks for their Egyptian taskmasters. Of course, we also eat lots of matzoh, the crackerlike, unleavened bread reminiscent of the haste with which the Israelites left Egypt. During the entire week of Pesach, to reinforce the experience of the Exodus, the other baked foods we eat are made with ground matzohs in the form of meal and don't use the normal types of leavening. It is not easy to forgo familiar foods for a week, but it is an important part of the holiday, reminding us of both our precious Jewish heritage and of the lessons of the festival.

A fascinating further part of seder ritual was added toward the end of the Middle Ages: Elijah's Cup. Middle European Jews revived the belief in the coming of a Jewish messiah, to be led in by the prophet Elijah who, according to the Bible, had never died but had been drawn up to heaven in a whirlwind. Elijah's Cup was added to the center of the table, empty until the end of the seder, then filled with wine as an offering for the reappearance of Elijah with the messiah. Directed by the haggadah, the door is left open for Elijah, and any hungry person, Jewish or otherwise, is welcome to come in.

The third of the Pilgrim Festivals is Shavuot, which occurs seven weeks after Pesach. This holiday commemorates the giving of the Torah on Mount Sinai. Reform Jews have created a wonderful modern ritual for this day. On Shavuot, those high school students who have completed three years of religious school beyond their Bar Mitzvah (boys) or Bat Mitzvah (girls) celebrate Confirmation. As a class, they confirm their Jewish education and their Jewish faith. Often this takes the form of an original service that is presented by the entire group. Confirmation is one of my favorite moments in the Jewish year. I appreciate the effort it takes to continue Jewish education beyond Bar or Bat Mitzvah; I find the service presented by the confirmands very moving.

A SENSE OF HISTORY

Judaism provides me with a strong connection to my past. Each of the holidays described above has its own historical framework. The three Pilgrim Festivals remind me of a time when Jews lived in their own land and, as a community, ascended the hills to Jerusalem where they gathered in the Holy Temple and offered thanks for the bounty of the land. To us in a modern community almost completely divorced from agriculture, these festivals recall that ancient way of life. Whenever I hear our customary Pesach recitation—"In every generation, we must think of ourselves as though we, too, had gone out from Egypt"—I imagine myself pausing at the shore of the Red Sea, fearful of taking that first step into the water, or standing at the foot of Mount Sinai, waiting for Moses to return with the Torah. I do not believe that every event in the Bible took place, but I still identify with those moments of Jewish history. Similarly, I feel akin to the Jews of medieval Spain who used the resources of their adopted land to create an entire world of Jewish literature and philosophy. I also feel the pain of countless Jews, pursued and persecuted for their beliefs and way of life. And so it goes; my Jewish connection transcends time and space. I feel proud to be a link in a tradition that spans thousands of years and shall continue for thousands more.

DIVERSITY AND UNITY WITHIN
THE JEWISH COMMUNITY

Even as I describe Jewish holidays or life-cycle ceremonies, I am mindful that my particular brand of observance and belief is not shared by all Jews. As a liberal Jew, I glory in the diversity of the Jewish community. In a manner of speaking, there are as many ways to be a Jew as there are Jews. And that, to me, is both one of the great strengths of Judaism and the assurance of its survival. Throughout our history there has been diversity in practice and degree, although

I think it is safe to say that modernity has brought the greatest amount of change. Some Jews are strictly observant, believing that the Torah is the actual word of God, handed down through Moses to the people of Israel. For those Jews, all the commentaries and codifications of the Torah were given to Moses as well. Other Jews do not consider themselves religiously observant at all; instead, they feel a strong cultural or nationalistic bond with their fellow Jews. Their tie to Judaism may come through identification with the state of Israel or through Jewish culture—music, art, literature. Our Jewish identity is an amalgam of many kinds of Jewish associations.

For example, I identify myself as a religiously observant Reform Jew with strong ties to Israel. As a Reform Jew, I believe that I have the responsibility to choose the extent to which Judaism plays an active role in my life. As a rabbi, that extent is pretty clear. As I noted earlier, I define time in Jewish terms. I celebrate Jewish holidays and special life-cycle events. I make ethical choices based on Jewish values. An important distinction, however, is that I make these choices based on a personal sense of commandment. Yet my version of Jewish life would not be acceptable to most traditional Jews. I must choose the Jewish way of life that is right for me, armed with as great a knowledge of the whole range of tradition as possible. As a rabbi, I try to teach my community that their Jewish decisions should be made with informed choice. This is the strength of Reform Judaism, and this is its challenge as well. Without any absolutes, it is far too easy to choose to do nothing, and rationalize that Reform Judaism says it is acceptable to make this decision. To challenge this misconception remains one of my principal objectives as a rabbi.

One of the problems inherent in the diversity of Jewish practice and identity is the threat to Jewish unity. A sense of k'lal yisrael, the unity of the Jewish people, is of major importance to our common survival. Because we differ on so many issues, we must find creative ways to retain our integrity as a people. A very personal example is that of women rabbis. Traditional Orthodox Judaism teaches that women fulfill a crucial role in the maintenance of the Jewish home, but their family obligations leave them without the needed flexibility to fulfill commandments governed by time; for example, praying each day at a fixed time. Home and children are surely a sacred responsibility but I do not believe that either women or men should be limited to any single area of life. In a time when caring for home and children precluded participation in communal life, that delineation of obligations may have made sense; today we have the means to include everyone in the totality of Jewish life. That inclusion extends to Jewish leadership. The Reform, Reconstructionist, and Conservative movements of Judaism agree with that assessment. Any Jew who fulfills the specific requirements of study and communal leadership earns the title of rabbi. For more than fifteen years now, women have been ordained and, while their path has not been without obstacles, women rabbis have done much to change the face of modern Judaism. We have begun to think about many of the issues once taken for granted, such as using male terminology to describe God.

SANCTIFYING TIME

As a rabbi, one of the greatest responsibilities I have is to emphasize the importance of sanctifying time. In a world where the days rush by, one of our most common rhetorical questions is, Where did the time go? We really do not know the answer. Hours melt into days, days into weeks, and so on. Judaism commands us to acknowledge the passage of time by stopping to mark significant occasions.

The celebration of our holidays and festivals fulfills that commandment. And one of those most significant occasions occurs each week when we pause for Shabbat, the sabbath, our day of rest. Shabbat begins at sunset on Friday evening, as do all Jewish holidays, and continues until Saturday at sundown. To order our week as God ordered the first week—"in six days, God created the heaven and the earth, and on the seventh day, God rested"—is a prime mandate for all of us. The observance of Shabbat varies greatly among Jews, from strict following of all the rules and regulations set down by the sages, to a family dinner with the blessings for candles, bread, and wine. What is crucial, at least to me, is that Shabbat be acknowledged in some way as a time of reflection, a cessation of labor. The lesson of Shabbat is to recognize that the hurried rhythm of our lives needs to be slowed down each week.

We sanctify other important occasions with ceremonies for the significant life-cycle events in our lives. The Torah commands us to welcome each newborn boy into the community of the Jewish people with the rite of circumcision, called *brit milah*, according to the millennia-old covenant God made with Abraham. This ceremony does not make the baby Jewish; rather, it affirms the baby's Jewishness and is the official welcome into the Jewish people. During the ceremony, the child is given a Hebrew name, usually as a loving memorial to a relative who has died. This ceremony enhances the feeling of awe that accompanies the birth of the child. To glory in the wonder of new life, to reaffirm the continuity of the generations with the sharing of a name, and to welcome a new generation of the Jewish people are all part of holiness. I can bear witness to such feelings in my own life. When I stood in front of the open ark with my husband and newborn son, and heard my senior rabbi and friend offer blessings of welcome for that new life, I was aware of the joy and holiness of that moment.

One of the most important ways liberal Judaism responds to modernity is with the evolution of new life-cycle ceremonies. Brit milah is a significant moment of welcome for male babies but, until recently, Judaism had no corresponding sacred moment for welcoming girls. Traditionally, the father of the baby girl would be called to the Torah for an *aliyah* (blessings that accompany the Torah reading) and the baby's birth and name would be acknowledged. Neither the mother nor the new baby was present. Most liberal Jews saw this as an inequity. Over the past fifteen years a wide variety of new ceremonies have evolved to rectify the situation, each conveying that same sense of *kedusha* (holiness) as our traditional rituals.

I feel that same sense of awe when I stand with a bride and groom under the *huppah* (wedding canopy) or when I bless a thirteen-year-old who has just become a Bar Mitzvah or Bat Mitzvah. On one level these are ordinary moments—a man and woman get married, a child enters adolescence—but on another, more transcendent level, these are the most precious moments of life, worthy of special recognition.

OUR REGARD FOR GOD'S CREATION
AND CREATURES

Judaism teaches us that we are all created in the image of God: a spark of the divine rests within each one of us. We are commanded to keep this in mind as we interact with the world. The way we treat friends and family, the way we conduct business, the way we regard our environment should all be motivated by our recognition of God's place in our world.

The Torah teaches that the children of Israel stood at the foot of Mount Sinai as Moses forged a covenant with God on their behalf. Our tradition suggests that all of us met at Sinai—those who were actually there and the generations yet unborn. As a result, each of us feels personally bound in our covenantal relationship with God.

The philosopher Martin Buber taught that life exists in meeting, that is, in the encounter between people and the encounter between people and their environment. When we are able to exist in true relationship—seeing other people as they really are and not just for their use to us—then, and only then, can we have meaningful relationships. This is not easy to accomplish; we are much too often aware of what people can do for us rather than who they are to us. When we do have those rare moments of true meeting, we are exhilarated, not only by the joy inherent in that relationship but also by the certain knowledge that God is present with us as well.

This sense of God's presence in our relationships is beautifully expressed in a verse from a prayer by Rabbi Chaim Stern, the primary liturgist of the Reform movement:

> I swear that one and one are three
> I see it always so
> when lovers kiss
> and friends embrace.
> —*Gates of Forgiveness,*
> Central Conference of
> American Rabbis

In these reflections I have tried to share the essence of what makes Judaism so meaningful in my life and in the lives of the people with whom I work. To live a life marked by joyful celebration, sacred introspection, significant study, and ethical consideration is a privilege I try not to take for granted. To be part of a covenant people, a partner with God in the work of creation which renews itself every day is itself a sacred responsibility. And to have been offered the gift of sharing even a fraction of Judaism's importance with you evokes these words of thanksgiving: Blessed are You, Adonai our God, Ruler of the Universe, Who has kept us alive, sustained us and brought us to this moment of joy. Amen.

3

CATHOLICISM

ROBERT A. ORSI

THE ORIGINS OF THE
CATHOLIC WAY

"Who do people say I am?" Jesus once asked the men and women who had been walking with him and listening to his teaching. He knew that people were struggling to understand him and that there were already many different answers to his question. His disciples answered, "John the Baptist; but others say, Elijah; and others, that one of the prophets has risen" (Luke 9:18–20). For the people of Galilee, who saw and touched this carpenter's son, the great challenge of understanding who he was had begun—a challenge that still has not ended some two thousand years later.

The first answers to the question came out of the faith and language of the Jewish community Jesus was born into, lived in, and addressed during the years of his public ministry. In the accounts of Jesus' life and teachings, written down after this death, some fifty titles are used to describe him, including "Son of Man," "Son of David," and "Messiah," all of them borrowed from Jewish tradition. Jesus understood himself in this tradition and presented himself to his people in ways they could understand.

His message was simple. When you pray, he told the people, ad-

Robert A. Orsi, Ph.D., is Associate Professor of Religious Studies at Indiana University, Bloomington, Indiana. He has served as Assistant Professor of Religious Studies at Fordham University, and was a Fulbright lecturer in American Studies at the University of Rome. He is the author of *The Madonna of 115th Street: Faith and Community in Italian Harlem, 1880–1950*.

dress God as "Abba," which was the Aramaic word for "Father." He told them that the Kingdom of God was at hand and that they must learn to live with each other in new and different ways. Like the prophets, he had a special love for the poor and the sick; he proclaimed that they would be the ones to inherit the Kingdom of Heaven. Jesus challenged men and women to become his disciples, and thus to dedicate themselves to God's service.

For teaching these things in the complex political and social world of Palestine, Jesus was executed as a common criminal. Stunned and frightened by what had happened to their teacher, Jesus' followers gathered together. In the days immediately following his crucifixion, these men and women realized that death had no power over their beloved teacher, that though he had died, he had risen again and was again among them. Catholics continue to express this faith at mass when they say they believe that Jesus "suffered, died, and was buried. On the third day he rose again, in fulfillment of the Scriptures; he ascended into heaven and is seated at the right hand of the father."

Jesus' followers continued to live as good and pious Jews, going to worship in the synagogue and then meeting among themselves to remember and celebrate their teacher. But gradually, the two communities grew apart. Christians began to keep Sunday, the first day of the week, as their special time for worship; and they changed the time of their gatherings from sunset to sunrise, a way of saying that with Jesus a new day had begun. Under the guidance of Paul of Tarsus, a devout Jew who had been converted to a deep faith in Jesus and who believed that Jesus had come to proclaim his message to the whole world, the earliest Christians began to welcome Gentiles, that is, non-Jews, into their midst. Thus the requirement that Gentiles conform to Jewish customary law before they could become Christians was eventually abandoned.

A CONCRETE FAITH

As the story of Jesus' life spread throughout the cities of the Roman Mediterranean world, a special problem arose. The men and women who believed in Jesus' extraordinary mission on earth were confronted with a difficult question: What was Jesus' relationship with God the Father? Some Jews said he was the Messiah, but not God; Greeks, who could not understand the concept of a god dying, said that Jesus only took on the appearance of a human being, only appearing to suffer and die, but that really he was all god. Others said that he was a messenger of God.

But one group of his followers, the earliest Christians, the men and women who had walked through Palestine with Jesus and who gathered to remember him after his death, insisted that Jesus was both human and divine. This, they claimed, was the faith of the men and women who knew Jesus, and this was the faith they wanted preserved. They insisted on Jesus' humanity: he was really born, of a real woman; he really lived and ate and breathed; and he really suffered and died. Their insistence on Jesus' divinity gave rise to another question: How could there be only one God, which was their belief, if in some way Jesus was also divine? In response to this question the doctrine of the Trinity developed. According to Catholic teaching, God, Jesus, and the Holy Spirit are one — one God. The Holy Spirit is God always present in the work of the church in its mission on earth; Jesus is God made present and visible to men and women in history.

The insistence on Jesus' humanity has been characteristic of the Catholic tradition throughout its history. Saint Francis of Assisi gave expression to it when, in the early thirteenth century, he created the first Christmas créche showing an infant Jesus surrounded by farm animals in a stable. It is revealed in the busts of the suffering Jesus found in many Catholic churches. And it is expressed in general in the familiarity and closeness Catholics feel with the sacred: they talk to Jesus, his mother, Mary, and the saints, carry pictures of them in their wallets, and plead with them to help them with the difficulties of their lives. They even tell humorous stories about the saints.

Thus, Catholics have a strong sense of Jesus' real presence among them. They believe he is really there in the church and its sacraments, and that he welcomes all men and women to come to him. They also believe that their leaders have a special link with this living Jesus. Catholics say that Jesus appointed the apostles to lead the church, and in particular that he made Peter head of the whole church. (The story of Peter's appointment and special place in the community of Jesus' followers is told in Matt. 16:15–20.) In turn, the apostles trusted their authority to their successors, and so on through history. This means that the pope and the bishops stand as the most recent representatives of an authority that stretches back to Jesus and the apostles, a human chain linking the present to the days of Jesus' life. This is called the *doctrine of apostolic succession*.

Thus Catholicism is a concrete faith attaching significance to humanity as well as divinity. It is not surprising then that the Catholic tradition has always valued this world, with all its beauty and potential, while at the same time looking forward to its completion and fulfillment in paradise. Catholic faith is a vivid and sensuous faith, expressing itself in color, music, stone, incense, and light.

THE CHURCH AND THE WORLD

Another expression of the concreteness of Catholic faith has been the way Catholics live in society. At first there was a sharp tension between the church and Roman society because Christians could not and would not participate in the rites that proclaimed the Roman emperor to be divine. Then, in 313 C.E., the emperor Constantine, who had just defeated all his rivals, ordered that Christianity was to have all the rights and privileges of other religions in the Empire. Eighty years later one of Constantine's successors, Theodosius I, declared Christianity the only legally recognized faith of the Roman world.

Constantine's interest in Christianity was mainly political at first. By the time of his victory over his rivals, the Christian churches had been securely disciplined and ordered under the authority of their bishops and were bound together by a common faith in Christ. Constantine and his successors, concerned to bring a new order to the lands of the Roman Empire, appreciated the social usefulness of the church and hoped that, by a close alliance with it, peace and public order could be reestablished. It seems that Constantine also developed a genuine love for Christ and consented to be baptized on his deathbed.

After the reign of Constantine, Catholics lived in the world in a new way. They looked to their political leaders to protect the rights and authority of the church; and they believed that the pope had important social and political authority. The popes were in fact political rulers as well as spiritual leaders. By the middle of the 700s, the papacy was in possession of the so-called Papal States, the sections of central Italy that were governed by the popes until the end of the nineteenth century. In the nineteenth and twentieth centuries, Cath-

olics began to change their understandings of the relationship between church and state. In the United States, for example, Catholics
realized that their church was one among many others, that all had
equal rights under the law, and that spiritual leaders had no special
relationship with the state.

Catholics still participate fully in the life and struggles of the world,
however, accepting their responsibility to work for justice and peace.
Throughout Latin America, for example, "base communities," small
groups of Catholics, gather together to promote the ideals of justice
and equality. Catholic theologians teach the "option for the poor,"
that is, that the poor have a special claim for the attention and concern of society. Many Catholic laypeople and their bishops are struggling against injustice and tyranny in many different societies
throughout the world.

A World Church

Since the time of Paul's journeys around the Mediterranean, Catholic
Christians have acted on their belief that Jesus' message is for all men
and women. The geography of the contemporary Catholic Church
reveals this: large Catholic communities can be found in North and
South America, Europe, Oceania, Africa, and Asia.

Among these many peoples and cultures, the struggle to understand Jesus—and to worship him in ways that are meaningful and
relevant to the different cultures—continues. It is a great challenge for
men and women not just in Africa or Asia, but also in the secular
cities of the industrially developed world, to understand a man who
lived and taught in ancient Palestine and who talked about and understood himself in the ancient philosophy and beliefs of the Jewish
people.

Catholics have responded to this challenge by imagining Jesus as
he would have appeared had he been born into their different cultures. In Africa, for example, Jesus is sometimes portrayed as a black
man; among Native Americans, he wears colorful ceremonial robes.
The Asian Catholic understanding is influenced by the rich spiritual
traditions of Buddhism and Hinduism. Poor people imagine Jesus as
one of them, and wherever Catholics have struggled for social justice
and peace, they have understood Jesus as struggling alongside of
them. In this way Jesus becomes real to Catholics of many different
races, cultures, and histories.

In many parts of the world Catholicism coexists with another ancient Christian religious tradition that is similar to it but also quite different and independent—the Orthodox tradition of Greece, Eastern Europe, and the Middle East. (These are the major historical centers of Orthodoxy; there are Orthodox churches in many other countries, including India, for example, and the United States.) The Orthodox respect the authority and teachings of the Roman Catholic church, but have their own leaders, called patriarchs, and their own theological and spiritual traditions. Perhaps most characteristic of Orthodox worship is the centrality of the icon, painted pictures of God and the saints. The Orthodox say that these are like windows opening onto the sacred, and they pray before them (not directly to them). Controversy over the meaning and use of such pictures combined with the geographical division of the Roman Empire into eastern and western halves and the behavior of Western European crusaders in the cities of the Eastern Empire drove the two churches bitterly apart. Today, however, the two traditions, together with the Anglican tradition, which also calls itself Catholic, are searching jointly for a new means of communication and sharing.

Tradition

On any street in Rome a visitor can see buildings dating from many different centuries, all still in use: a nineteenth-century office building next to a shoe-repair store operating in a seventeenth-century stable, next to a twelfth-century church. Similarly, the Catholic way combines many different aspects of a long history; nothing is ever lost or abandoned, but always adapted and used. A respect for history is an important part of the Catholic way. Catholics try to keep faith with the past as they face situations that demand new kinds of responses and ideas. They are in dialogue with the past as they address the present and the future.

A PEOPLE OF CELEBRATION

The Meaning of Worship

The Catholic way is a way of joyous celebration. Catholic people throughout the world proclaim who they are, what they believe, and what they love in festivals. Some celebrations are held on particular days of the year, when Catholics recall events in Jesus' life or in the lives of Mary, his mother, and the saints. Other celebrations, called *sacraments,* are held at special moments in a person's life. There are also celebrations unique to particular communities of Catholics in different parts of the world. Some European towns, for example, celebrate the feast days of their patron saints, whom they believe watch over and protect their communities.

On all these various occasions Catholics express their joy and love in color, song, and movement. They decorate their homes, churches, and neighborhoods with flowers and colored banners; in church they sing and play music appropriate to the occasion; they go on procession through the streets of their communities. At home on these wonderful days, they cook and eat special meals with friends and family. What is so special about these times? What do these moments mean? What does it mean when a Catholic worships his or her God?

Remembering, celebrating, participating, communicating—these words will help us to understand Catholic worship. In their festivals and sacraments, Catholics remember times and people important in their lives and in the life and history of their community. On Good Friday, for example, Catholics remember the suffering and death of Jesus on the cross, and on Easter they celebrate the triumph of his resurrection. On August 15, Catholics celebrate Mary's entry into heaven; and on March 17, Irish Catholics in North America march in the streets of their communities in honor of Saint Patrick, a missionary who brought Catholicism to Ireland in the fifth century.

Frequently Catholics will reenact the important moment they are recalling; and through their participation in that reenactment, the event of the past becomes present again. Participants lose track of place and time and feel a part of the event. That very experience occurs during Catholic sacraments, especially the Eucharist. As the priest and the congregation reenact important happenings in the history of the church, the moment becomes present again.

At such times Catholics express their gratitude for an event or a person important to them. In the joy, music, and companionship of their festivals they are saying that their lives were forever improved by what happened in the past. So their reenactment is ultimately a communication. They communicate with God, Jesus, Mary, and the saints; they communicate with the priests of their church; and they communicate with each other.

The past event that Catholics, as other Christians, most want to celebrate is Easter, the triumph of Jesus over human sinfulness and death. Considered the beginning of Christianity, Easter is the central event in the life of the church and, according to Catholics, in the history of the world. All Catholic festivals and sacraments, whatever else they are about, are primarily celebrations of this one great act.

The Seven Sacraments

According to Catholic teaching, a sacrament is a sign of God's grace and presence in the life of each individual and of the church. The word *sign* needs to be carefully understood here. Think of a person waving. The hand raised in greeting is a sign; but it is not only that: it is the nature of the greeting itself. The gesture is the accomplishment. So it is with Catholic sacraments. They are signs of God's presence and they are actual moments of that presence. God is, of course, present at other times or places, but in the sacraments God is present most visibly and clearly. Catholics have a special confidence that in the sacraments God is really present to them; and the source of this confidence is Jesus' promise that after his time on earth this is the way it would be.

There are seven sacraments: baptism, the Eucharist, confirmation, penance, matrimony, holy orders, and anointing of the sick. During each of these sacraments, something happens; each of them is an action, with a before and an after. The questions are, What happens during a sacrament? and To whom does it happen?

At the heart of the sacramental life of the Catholic church is the celebration of the Eucharist, the most important and vivid memory of the community. Shortly before Jesus died, during the Last Supper, the last meal he ate with his twelve disciples, he took the bread and wine that were on the table, blessed them, and gave them to the disciples. Catholics believe that what happened that night was uniquely important. Jesus knew that he was about to be killed, so he "took bread, and blessed and broke it, and gave it to the disciples and said 'Take, eat; this is my body.' And he took a cup, and gave it to them, saying, 'Drink of it, all of you; for this is my blood of the covenant, which is poured out for many for the forgiveness of sins' " (Matt.

26:26–28). Jesus' flesh and blood would be sacrificed for the redemption of the world. He invited his disciples to eat his flesh and blood — in other words, to share in his mission and prepare themselves to follow him even to their deaths, and he told them to remember him by recalling and repeating what he had done that night at the table.

From that evening on, the celebration of the Eucharist in Jesus' name and memory has been the central act of worship in the Catholic community. It is the expression of the unity of the church: whether only two people are present or two hundred thousand people, Catholics say that at each celebration of the Eucharist the whole church is present and in solidarity.

The Eucharist is also the church's special experience of the presence of Christ. Catholics believe that the Eucharist is a sacrifice: at each celebration, Jesus' sacrificial act on the cross, his offering of himself for the world, is repeated. Jesus took upon himself the sins of all mankind. So it is that, in the eucharistic celebration, Catholics repeatedly reenact what they consider to be the most important moment in human history: Jesus' sacrifice of himself afresh for the salvation of humanity. Catholics also believe that during the celebration of the Eucharist, through the actions and prayers of the priest and the people, the bread and wine on the altar are changed into the body and blood of Christ. This is the doctrine of the real presence; the process of the change is called *transubstantiation.*

Given the importance of the Eucharist in Catholicism, it would seem that all a Catholic has to do to be a good person and a faithful Catholic is to go to Mass. The Eucharist, however, is not thought of as a separate aspect of the Catholic way; going to Mass is not an isolated moment either in the life of an individual or in the life of the church. It is an ongoing celebration that takes place in the church of today as it exists in the world as it is. Catholics understand that the mission of their church in the world includes the struggle for justice and peace, a concern for the poor and sick, compassion for those in trouble. The Eucharist is the complete expression of all that is the Catholic faith. This means that a person who goes to Mass is committed to all the beliefs and all the activities the church is working for in the world; and Catholics say that during the Eucharist, celebrated in fellowship with others, an individual will receive new strength, purpose, and courage to do this work.

Sacraments then are signs of God's living presence and of the unity and identity of the church; and they are actions that enable, empower, and emphasize. They emphasize the responsibilities of being a Catholic, and they empower Catholics to meet those responsibilities in a spirit of solidarity with the church and confidence in Christ.

In the sacrament of baptism, an individual—usually an infant, although Catholics also appreciate the importance of adult baptism—is welcomed to the community of the church and to participation in the tasks of the church in the world. The sacrament of confirmation, most commonly administered to boys and girls of junior-high-school age, reinforces the invitation first given in baptism. In the sacrament of matrimony, the community of Catholics recognizes and celebrates the love that exists between a man and a woman, inviting the married couple to understand their love as another contribution to the work of the church in the world. The church's special ministers are anointed in the sacrament of holy orders.

Finally, in two sacraments the church seeks specifically to heal: in the sacrament of penance, commonly termed Confession, men and women who are sorry for their sins are reconciled with the community of Catholics, who always remember that they too are liable to sin and are always in need of mercy and compassion. In the sacrament of the anointing of the sick, men and women who are suffering physically are prayed for by the church, are reminded that they remain members of the community of Catholics, and are invited to follow Jesus in offering their suffering as a sacrifice for the good of their fellows.

Knowledge of the sacraments and their significance, among other information, is conveyed to adult converts to Catholicism in a course of study lasting approximately a year which is named the Rite of Christian Initiation of Adults.

Popular Celebrations and the
Church Calendar

Sacraments are also the occasions of great family celebrations. When a child is baptized, for example, family and friends gather to celebrate the event. The day is completed with the finest and most generous meal the family can provide. This same spirit characterizes Catholic celebrations of major holy days.

The two great seasons of the Catholic year are centered around Christmas and Easter. A period of waiting precedes both holidays. Advent, which begins on the fourth Sunday before Christmas, is the time when Catholics, together with other Christians, prepare themselves for the day they will remember and celebrate, the birth of Jesus. It is an exciting time, full of anticipation, consistent with how a family feels as the birth of a longed-for child approaches. The other important season of the church year is Lent, the time that begins on Ash Wednesday, forty days before Easter, and continues through to Easter. Forty days beyond is the celebration of the day of Christ's ascension into heaven (Ascension Day, Ascension Thursday).

Lent begins as a solemn and somber time, with the priest uttering the words, "Remember that you are dust and unto dust you will return," as he makes a small cross of ashes on the foreheads of Catholics on Ash Wednesday. It culminates in the celebrations of Holy Week that begin on Palm Sunday, the Sunday before Easter. In Catholic churches throughout the world the account of Jesus' passion, as his suffering and death are called, is read during the Eucharist, and palms are distributed. These branches recall the palms that the people of Jerusalem spread before the feet of Jesus' donkey as he entered Jerusalem for the last time on the way to his death. Thursday of Holy Week is called Holy Thursday, at which time Catholics, along with most other Christians, recall the events of the night that Jesus was taken prisoner. Friday is known as Good Friday, the most solemn day of the Catholic year: the churches are still, no bells are rung, the altars are kept bare and without flowers, and a mood of sorrow fills the people as they recall Jesus' passion. This mood gives way to the exhilarating explosion of color, sound, fire, and joy at midnight on Easter Sunday as the church recalls Christ's triumph over death.

Lent is a serious time when people are encouraged to think about how they have been living, about whether they have furthered or hindered God's work of love and peace in the world. Lent is also a penitential time when people reflect on the difficulties of being disciples of Jesus. Yet Catholics never forget that, in fact, Jesus has already triumphed over death. Even in the seriousness of Lent, the dominant note is hope. People sometimes think that Advent is the joyous season, Lent the sad one; but really both are joyous because the church lives in the time after Easter, and all its memories are touched by what happened that day.

Easter in the Orthodox churches does not coincide with the Catholic Easter. Instead, it falls from one to five weeks later. The different timing is in accordance with the movable date of the Jewish Passover and its relation to the Last Supper. The events of Holy Week in the Orthodox churches are generally similar to those in the Catholic church, but somewhat expanded and more ornate.

Besides these two great seasons, Catholics celebrate a number of other holidays throughout the year: January 1, when Jesus' circumcision is recalled; January 6, Epiphany, which celebrates the arrival of the Magi in Bethlehem; March 25, the day of the Annunciation, which commemorates Mary's discovery that she would bear the Christ child; November 1, called All Saints' Day; and December 8, the feast of the Immaculate Conception, which celebrates Mary's own sinlessness. Others, called movable feasts, fall on different days each year. The most important of them are Ascension Thursday; Pentecost, the seventh Sunday after Easter, which recalls the day following Christ's ascension into heaven when his apostles determined with the guidance and assistance of the Holy Spirit to proclaim Christ's teachings in the streets of Jerusalem; and the great springtime feast of Corpus Christi that proclaims Christ as Lord.

To assist them in worship, Catholics use candles, holy water, holy oils, and statues and medals that depict Jesus, Mary, and the saints. Many Catholics use a rosary to guide their prayers—this is a circle of beads, arranged in groups of ten, with a space between each group and an additional bead in each space. The prayer called the Hail Mary is recited for each of the ten beads, followed by the recitation of the Lord's Prayer for each of the beads in the spaces. In many churches a series of fourteen pictures or small sculptures, known as the Stations of the Cross, depicting Jesus' passion, line the wall. These are important in the prayer lives and worship of some Catholics who, moving from image to image, recall Jesus' passion and say special prayers for their intentions and for the work of the church.

Catholics around the world have found ways of worshiping God with gestures and objects that have meaning in their individual native cultures. In India, for example, bells constitute an important part of the liturgy; in Africa, drums and dance are used to express the people's faith. The various cultures that make up the universal Catholic church have different ways of celebrating important feast days. Latin Americans, for example, on Good Friday, publicly reenact Jesus' passion in the streets of their communities. In many cultures pilgrimages to special sacred places are an important way of celebrating holy days. In Italy a particular kind of bread is baked and distributed on March 19, the feast of Saint Joseph. There is great diversity in the Catholic way, although there is an even greater unity.

The Special Place of Mary in Catholic Worship

To many people, the most obvious characteristic of the Catholic way is the special place the Virgin Mary, Mother of Jesus, occupies in Catholic history, worship, and imagination. Her image, in its many different expressions, adorns Catholic churches around the world: as *theotokos,* or "bearer of God," she is depicted as a regally dressed empress, most often in Sicilian and Venetian churches and in churches adhering to the Orthodox and Byzantine traditions. Universally, Mary can be seen as the Immaculate Conception, shown treading on the head of Satan portrayed as a serpent; and as the Virgin of Sorrow she is shown mourning the body of her son. Perhaps the most popular and beloved image of Mary is simply the one of her as the Madonna, cradling the infant Jesus in her arms.

This image of Mary and Jesus together suggests the meaning of Mary in the church. Catholics do not worship Mary; worship is reserved for God alone. They love her, however, because, sacrificing herself, she freely accepted God's summons to bear the Messiah; her courageous Yes to this call prepared the way for Jesus' birth. She is thought of as the first Christian: her love for Jesus and her participation in the sorrows and challenges of his mission make her a model of what all Christians strive to be—faithful disciples of Jesus. Some Catholics believe that Mary expresses the mercy of God, and they pray to her to intercede for them with her son.

Mary is also seen by Catholics as a model of the church itself. Her faith, obedience, humility, cooperation, generosity, and mercy are all qualities that the church tries to project as it goes about the work of Christ in the world.

MONKS AND NUNS IN THE
CATHOLIC TRADITION

Sometime around 271 C.E., a young Egyptian Christian named Anthony gave his possessions to the poor and went into the desert to be alone with his God. The story of his sacrifices and struggles, recorded by a follower, in time became known throughout the church and inspired other young men and women to follow his example. The deserts of Egypt and Palestine were soon filled with monks, as this new sort of Christian came to be called. The word *monk* comes from the Greek word *monos*, which means "alone."

This story has been repeated in the modern world. In 1948, Thomas Merton, a young American who had also abandoned a full life in the world to live as a monk, wrote about his decision. His publisher, thinking that such a strange way of life would have little appeal to modern Americans, decided to print only two thousand copies of the first edition of the book, which was called *The Seven Storey Mountain*. In its first year, Merton's autobiography sold over six hundred thousand copies, and it is still in demand.

Early Monasticism

A monk lives an austere and severely disciplined life of work and prayer. Alone and silent for much of the time, a monk or a nun, as women monastics came to be called, seeks to worship and love God in constant prayer. (The Latin word for monk is *nonnus*, the feminine of which is *nunne*, whence "nun" is derived.) Why would a man or a woman choose to live such a life? And what accounts for the continued vitality of monasticism throughout the history of the Catholic tradition? The monastic life satisfies a particular longing some Catholic Christians have for an intimate relationship with God. All Catholics are called to this relationship. Most choose to live it in other ways, but this is the way monks and nuns desire.

The first monks and nuns, in the time of Anthony, were inspired by the examples of the martyrs who had gone to their deaths for refusing to pay homage to Roman gods. In their sufferings as they neared death, the martyrs seemed to experience a special closeness with Jesus, an intimacy that had previously been reserved for the apostles who had lived with him. Many of the martyrs claimed to see Jesus and talk with him at the moment of their deaths, and accounts of the martyrs' last moments were told and cherished throughout the early church.

After Constantine became emperor of the Roman Empire in 306 C.E. and permitted Christians to worship in peace, the issue of martyrdom was closed. But men and women still longed for the kind of close contact with Jesus that the martyrs had enjoyed. This was the immediate spiritual inspiration for the popularity of the new, bloodless martyrdom of monasticism: the desire for a close relationship with God.

At first the monastic life was simple and severe. Living alone in the desert, the monks fasted and prayed, supporting themselves by crafts such as weaving baskets. In the silence and emptiness of the desert, they struggled with strange fantasies and desires, which today we might call delusions, and labored to fix their attention on one reality, God. In this they were following the teachings of a school of philosophy popular at the time that described the spiritual life as the flight of the alone to the Alone, the single self in relation to the single God.

As men and women filled the deserts in search of this encounter with their God, however, it soon became clear that some structure would have to be developed, some guidance given them in their quest. Pachomius, who lived in the deserts of southern Egypt, gathered his followers around him in a community and ordered their lives around shared prayer and work. When the monastic impulse, carried along trade routes into southern France, reached the West, Pachomius's work of organization was continued and perfected by Benedict of Nursia, the son of a Roman civil servant.

In a book entitled simply the *Rule,* Benedict outlined a structure for monastic life that remains the dominant model to this day. Every moment of time was accounted for by Benedict. Seven times a day the monks gathered to pray together; they ate together, worked and lived together, each moment of their days governed by the *Rule.* Benedict wanted the monks to live together in worship and prayer, and he muted the emphasis on heroic solitude popular in the East. He was a master organizer and his book, small enough to be easily copied and memorized, had an extraordinary impact on Western culture. As the institutions of society collapsed in Western Europe in the sixth and seventh centuries, little communities of men and women, gathered under the calm order and regularity of Benedict's *Rule,* offered islands of security and peace amidst turbulence. This was never the intention of the *Rule:* according to Benedict, the monk had one goal in life—to pray. Nevertheless, the strength of the order and discipline Benedict imposed spread far beyond the walls of the monasteries founded in his name.

The main purpose of the monastic life is still to pray, to live in communion with and service to God. Yet modern monks, like their medieval counterparts, cannot avoid the challenges of the world. For example, in the New York City area called Hell's Kitchen, a deteriorating and dangerous neighborhood, an ecumenical community of monks took over an abandoned building. Their intention was to establish a community of prayer, but the effect on the neighborhood has been profound. Spreading out from this center of hope and stability, a new life has come to this section of the city.

This has been the irony and strength of monasticism throughout the history of Catholicism: determined to go off to serve God, monks and nuns have found themselves forever challenged to serve God in serving humankind.

Catholic Sisters in the United States: Prayer and Action on America's Frontiers

Sisters, or nuns, have always lived wherever people need them the most. In the early 1800s, Catholic sisters worked among poor Irish immigrants in American cities. At the end of that century they helped the new Catholic immigrants from eastern and southern Europe. The sisters taught the immigrants and their children how to read and write, took care of the sick and dying, and gave shelter to orphans. During the Civil War, Catholic sisters in the North and the South earned a reputation for their excellent nursing abilities; they distributed food and medicine in the armies, cooked, worked in the military laundries, and risked their lives to bring care and comfort to wounded soldiers on the terrible battlefields of that war.

At first it was not clear how Catholic sisters, newly arrived from Europe, should live in the United States. In Europe most women religious led quiet lives of prayer and study in cloisters. Many decided to live this way in the United States as well. There are still American nuns living in cloisters today. Their primary activity is prayer, but they do other types of work as well, such as sewing the garments and cloths used in Catholic worship.

Other sisters decided that the turbulent conditions of life in the new republic required a more active engagement. They began an important tradition of action, service, and commitment that is now characteristic of American sisters. A good example is seen in the Sisters of Charity, an American congregation founded in 1809 by American Elizabeth Seton. The Sisters of Charity work in hospitals, orphanages, and schools. During the cholera epidemics of 1832–34, 1849–50, and 1855, they bravely tended the sick of all faiths, earning national praise. The Sisters of Charity are an important part of the American Catholic world.

At home and in the foreign missions, American Catholic sisters have always understood their work to be caring for the whole person, body and soul. They pray with the poor—and defend them in court and organize for their rights. They comfort the sick—and tend their bodies and build hospitals for them. American Catholic sisters are at home in many worlds, sacred and secular.

The last twenty years have been a time of change for American sisters. Their numbers have dwindled. Many are looking for new work challenges and fewer of them are going into teaching and nursing. The most obvious changes have to do with what sisters wear—the veils and habits of the past have almost disappeared, replaced by contemporary clothing—and where they live. Many sisters have moved out of their convents, preferring to live in small communities in apartments and houses. In all of these ways, American sisters responded to the challenge of the Second Vatican Council, which encouraged Catholics to go out into the world to live among and work with men and women of all faiths.

But American sisters remain faithful to their traditions of action and service. They work today as social workers and scientists, psychiatrists and community planners, scholars and labor organizers. American Catholic sisters have devoted themselves to the struggle for peace and social justice in the United States and around the world, with sometimes tragic results: in 1980 three American sisters and a young laywoman were killed by government troops in El Salvador where they were working among the poor and oppressed. But they continue to work in situations of great risk and danger, strong in their belief that this is where their religious faith requires them to be. Their education, devotion, and commitment have made these American sisters an important force for change in the modern Catholic Church.

A NEW CHURCH IN A NEW WORLD: ROMAN CATHOLICISM AFTER THE SECOND VATICAN COUNCIL

Angelo Roncalli became Pope John XXIII in 1958, a difficult time for the Roman Catholic church—and the world. For more than two centuries the church had steadfastly rejected the perspectives and assumptions of modern culture. Freud, Marx, and Darwin had posed intellectual threats that seemed to challenge the very foundations of Catholic belief. Modern movements like nazism and fascism denied the dignity and integrity of the human person.

In 1958 Catholic thinkers were wondering if there were some way that religious men and women could open a conversation with modern secular people to discover shared values and hopes. However justified the church's rejection of the modern world may have been at one time, many Catholics were afraid that if the church remained closed off from the world the vitality of the Catholic mission itself would become endangered.

The world at the moment seemed filled with hope and fear. The hope came from the beginning of Third World liberation with its promise of new freedom and democracy there, from the economic prosperity of the industrial nations, and from the great progress humankind seemed to have made in medical, industrial, and communications technologies. The fear came from the persistent threat of nuclear war between East and West. Was there some way the church could both learn from this complex situation and address it meaningfully with the voice of the Catholic tradition?

John XXIII thought there was. In 1959 he announced plans for a world Catholic council that would open in Rome in 1962. This meeting, known as the Second Vatican Council (the first was held in 1869–70), met from 1962 through 1965. First, under John's guidance and then, after his death in 1963, under Paul VI, the Council was dedicated to the ideal of *aggiornamento*, the "updating" of the church and its engagement with the modern world.

In a number of documents the Council set the agenda for Roman

Catholicism in the twentieth century. It committed Catholics to the struggle for social justice and recognized that in this work Catholics could share with and learn from men and women of different faiths. It opened the way for dialogue between Catholics and other Christians. The Council approved changes in the Catholic liturgy that would reflect this new spirit—Catholics now celebrate the Mass in their own languages rather than in Latin, and there is more congregational participation in the celebration than before.

The vision and ideals of the Second Vatican Council inspired and transformed the Catholic world. Since the Council, for example, the church in South and Central America has denied its traditional alliance with the rich and powerful classes and has dedicated itself to serving the poor in city slums and rural villages. In the United States, the National Conference of Catholic Bishops has issued important calls for an end to the nuclear arms race and for a more just distribution of American prosperity. Catholics around the world have evolved new forms of prayer and worship more congenial to their different cultural styles. Lay people have sought a more active role in the mission of the church.

The years since the Second Vatican Council have been exciting but also difficult. Catholics struggle to discover how to practice the values and beliefs of their tradition in a way that listens to the modern world when it has something to teach, and that criticizes it when necessary. But Catholics always strive to engage in open dialogue with men and women of good will in the modern world who share with Catholics the same concerns for peace, justice, and human dignity.

THE CHURCH AS THE PEOPLE OF GOD
ON PILGRIMAGE

It has been necessary to talk about the uniqueness of the Catholic way in order to enable the reader to understand it. But this should not be allowed to obscure the identity that Catholics share with all other Christians, regardless of how bitterly history has divided them. Catholics are at work on the mission of their Lord in the world; their church is a community of love and commitment. They look forward to the completion of their work at the end of time, when they believe Jesus will come again, but they also understand that they have been challenged by Christ to do God's will on earth. They can do their work because Jesus did his: he offered his life as a sacrifice for the redemption of the world. Catholics believe that in the present time, while they are about their work in the world, they have the Holy Spirit to guide them, to help them find the wisdom and love that the challenge of discipleship demands.

Together with other Christians—and indeed with all men and women who hunger and thirst after justice and peace—Catholics are pilgrims in the world. They go about their work in love: love of God and, in that love, love of their brothers and sisters. Rooted in tradition, challenged and enabled by Christ, accompanied by their leaders, they are at work on the great task Jesus called his followers to undertake.

4

EUCHARIST—
HEART OF MY FAITH

NAN MERRILL

Much of my life has been a search for that faith community in which I could have the beautiful experience of coming home. Something—or perhaps more accurately, someone—has been drawing me "home" since I was a child. As early as I can remember, I have felt the presence of angels. Yet the angel that companioned me during my long hospitalization with polio at five years of age was dismissed by others as childish imagination. Slowly I learned to live quietly with my unseen guests and to live with the confusion of why angels were so acceptable in the Bible but not in real life.

I remember feeling pangs of jealousy when I saw my classmates preparing to make their First Communions, dressed in white like young brides, and, after that, when they were free (though they often complained) to go to confession. So often I felt guilty and wished I, too, could go and tell my "sins" to someone and be forgiven. After attending the Sunday school my parents sent me to, I would sometimes walk to the Catholic church and sit on the steps or even sneak into the back of the church to see and to hear the Mass. Despite the use of Latin, of which I understood not a word, the power of the Eucharist was somehow conveyed to me through the ritual, the icons, the vigil lights, and, as I would now understand it, through the cu-

Nan Merrill, a layperson active in the Roman Catholic church, is a graduate of the Foundation for Religion and Mental Health in Briarcliff, N.Y., and the Guild for Spiritual Guidance in Rye, N.Y. She has been a lay pastoral minister; the editor of *Friends of Silence*, a monthly journal of interfaith messages for peace, understanding, and reflections; and a retreat facilitator.

mulative faith and hearts of those receiving the body and blood of Christ. For that is the heart of the Catholic faith.

There followed a long period of wandering in the desert, discovering an oasis here and there, yet never feeling at home . . . dry years of trying to live on my own resources with very little spiritual sustenance. Then, in my early thirties, I found myself rising each night when everyone else was asleep and staring at one particular star, offering out a silent, unworded cry to whomever it may concern. After months of this prayer of unknowing, I awakened one morning to a new world—to what I can only describe as living in the love of God. This seeming to dwell in heaven on earth for the next ten days was as if a veil had been lifted from my very being and I was experiencing my true birthright. When the "veil" fell once again, I knew beyond a doubt that there was a deeper, wider, higher way to live, and that I would never be satisfied until I could live in that love.

Had I known then the long and painful journey on which I had rather naively embarked, I wonder if I would have stepped out. Yet, mercifully, we have only to take one step at a time; we do not have to know the end of the journey. And, since that prayer of unknowing was answered so unexpectedly and in such a loving and surprising way, life has become for me anticipation, expectation, mystery, wonder, and surrender. The journey has not been without much sacrifice and suffering. Yet I could make no other. And at each crossroad, I have been gifted with individuals who could point the direction to the next path on the way.

Three important steps in my coming home to the Catholic faith were crucial. First, I became program coordinator for the Guild for Spiritual Guidance, a two-year training program for professionals in New York. There I was introduced to the mystics and saints through a study of the Christian tradition. Each one became my sister, my brother, my friend. Even though I had on many occasions prayed to and through a few saints that, as a Protestant, I had "met" through Catholic friends, I never dreamed of the rich heritage and guidelines to the spiritual life available through reading about their lives. Then when Dan Berrigan came to the guild for five sessions, I cried my way through his talks. He could have been saying "fish for sale," and it would have been as awakening for me. For I knew I was sitting in the presence of someone whose life was the outward sign of his inner-faith journey. I sensed through his sharing that to receive daily Eucharist is, in some mysterious way, to become Eucharist and therefore a more beneficial person in and for the world. His way-of-being in the world opened the door of my heart to peace and justice through social action. I hungered for more.

Then, Edward Farrell, another cultivator at the guild, introduced us to the Prayer of Abandonment out of the spirituality of Charles de Foucauld. De Foucauld (1858–1916) was born to a distinguished family, then orphaned, raised to an army career, and discharged early for dissolute conduct. Reversing his dissipation, he joined the French Foreign Legion, regained his rank, and was honored for bravery. Leaving the army and returning to the Sahara for exploration, he was servant to a rabbi, became a Trappist monk and then a Catholic priest. De Foucauld was also impressed by the faith of Muslims at prayer and lived among them for a number of years before his assassination by fanatics during a revolt against France. Posthumously, his writings inspired the establishment of three communities of hermits: the Little Brothers of Jesus, the Little Sisters of Jesus, and, later, the Little Brothers and Sisters of the Eucharist.

When I heard de Foucauld's Prayer of Abandonment, I knew I had found the prayer of my heart, the prayer I had unknowingly awaited:

> Father [though I prefer Beloved of my heart], I abandon myself into your hands; do with me what you will. I am ready for all; I accept all. Let only your will be done in me and in all your creatures; I wish no more than this, O Lord. Into your hands I commend my soul. Do with it what you will. For I love you, Lord, and so need to give myself, to surrender myself into your hands, without reserve and with boundless confidence, for you are my Father [Beloved of my heart]. Amen.

I began each morning with this prayer, and each evening, often stumbling through it, not yet recognizing its power working in me.

A few months after faithfully praying the Prayer of Abandonment, I made a three-week, silent, semifasting retreat at a Benedictine monastery. For the first time I was able to participate fully and daily in the Eucharist. I discovered an insatiable hunger for the Eucharist in those three weeks. In fact, the daily schedule of praying, working, being at the monastery was so natural and satisfying for me that I became embarrassed, fearing that I would be seen as trying to "outdo" the monks. I was compelled to follow their rule of life as my own, and so grateful that I was allowed to do so. After this retreat I began to take formal instruction in the Catholic faith, and within a year had made my profession of faith. I finally came to live in my particular spiritual home.

However, even that was not easy to discern. I did not feel in harmony with the church's stand on several issues, such as the non-priesthood of women and denying the Eucharist to believers from all other different traditions. In exploring these seeming disharmonies, I went to see the priory master at another monastery (a three-hour drive I often took—so great was my hunger). There, although a Protestant, I could freely partake of Eucharist. His words to me were few, yet they made all the difference. He said, "If I were facing the decision you are trying to make today, I would assuredly say yes. Yet, I could only say my yes as a dissenter for the *upbuilding* of the church." And so I said my yes—a yes that draws me to the Communion table each day so that I might be drawn ever more deeply into Christ as I receive his body and blood into my body and blood, so that I shall recognize his hidden presence in all of my brothers and sisters. Through this experience, I know the power of Eucharist; I know I am always in need of Eucharist. So to share what it means for me to be of the Catholic faith is to share my experience of the Mass . . . of Eucharist.

The first time I made the sign of the cross over myself with others at a Mass, I felt the mystery of that unity of all of us being present with God. I promised myself I would never allow this symbol of being one with God in my mind, one with Christ in my heart, and one with the Holy Spirit in my soul to become routine. For out of this recognition of being in union with God, I can then greet others in community; I recognize we are all the family of God.

As a member of God's family, I am free to acknowledge my weaknesses, my brokenness. My childhood need for confession is fulfilled daily in the liturgy when I confess to God and to all my brothers and sisters that I have missed the mark. Each day this penitential rite offers me the opportunity to review my life, to recognize where I have failed to live to my fullest potential, to ask forgiveness of the Lord and from the community, and to receive new life. Even as my heart absorbs the words of my mouth, "Lord have mercy," I feel myself being loved into newness as I am born anew each day. When I am able to fully enter into confession with all my heart, whether it be the individual sacrament of reconciliation or a communal rite, I am led to conversion. I am changed. I feel blessed and at peace.

And my natural response is praise—Glory to God in the Highest! Even on those occasions when I have not fully accepted God's forgiveness, when I am unable to forgive myself, I am still free to praise God through my own lived faith and through the faith of the community gathered together. I am prepared and more open to hear and to receive the Word of Scripture so that I can answer the call to become a Word of God.

Reading, speaking, and listening to God's Word each day is essential to my growth in faith, essential to remembering who I am and whose I am. The voices of the prophets, the faith-story of God's people, the words of Jesus are just as relevant today as when they were first spoken. Through Scripture I hear Jesus asking me to feed his hungry sheep, to be his hands and feet, to carry his love to the brokenhearted, to be his light in the world. What he said to the Pharisees, to the woman at the well, to his disciples, to the woman convicted of adultery, to the thief beside him on the cross, he says to me. My response to his word is to live out the profession of my faith as best I can from day to day, through prayer, and becoming more of whom he calls me to be.

All of the Mass is a preparation for Eucharist, for that most reverent and holy time of receiving Christ's gift of himself into myself. Here I shall offer a confession to you, the reader, of an unexpected answer from me to women being denied priesthood and, therefore, denied the privilege of offering others the gift of Eucharist. At each and every Mass, I am compelled to concelebrate silently with the presiding priest. I did not think this out as a way to balancing masculine/feminine energy or to have a quiet rebellion. No, rather, I began to awaken frequently at night in the midst of celebrating Mass in my dreams, until I quite naturally found the words of blessing, the prayer over the gifts, the eucharistic prayer itself . . . welling up in me during the Mass each day. I cannot not participate as fully as is possible, though I have no desire to be seen or to offend anyone performing as a concelebrant. I share this because I believe my experience is not unique, that many women are prophets of what the church will live into in the next century.

Perhaps my offering myself so totally in each Eucharist is an appropriate response of gratitude for the many blessings in my life. Jesus consecrated his own life in the Eucharist and is always calling us to be with him, to do what he did and more. So, at each Eucharist, I have the opportunity—if I have the ability to respond—to affirm that I am a sacrament, that Jesus is the secret gift within me just waiting to be shared as his presence in the world, his present to the world. I speak for myself, but, of course, I mean everyone!

Eucharist also invites me to enjoy and cooperate with the company of heaven—so natural to me as a child. Angels abound as realities—from our guardian angels to the highest archangels of heaven to the angel of our church. To be Catholic is to be one who celebrates. Every week offers one or more feast days to remember a saint and to call forth the special qualities of that saint into our own lives. And I love celebrating one another on our respective feast days and of having my own saint, Anne de Beaupré, as a blessing. Along with the angels and saints, we pray each day for the heavenly community of those who have gone before us. Having always been aware of the ongoing "presence" of family members and friends who had died, acknowledging continued fellowship with them through prayer and Eucharist is sheer joy for me!

Eucharist also invites me to journey with Mary, who has become a companioning presence with me, the feminine model of whom I am called to become. I am humbled by her total surrender in faith to God, her gentleness, her fidelity to life even at the cross, her grace, peace, and compassion. I need her feast days as reminders that I am called to be as Mary to others. Though I love Mary, praying the rosary did not come naturally. At first, like praying the Stations of the Cross, I felt the rosary artificial, and I could not pray either of them alone. As I became more familiar with the prayers, I discovered that each of them brought me into the mystery of love. To pray the Stations of the Cross, especially during Lent, has been for me a powerful preparation for Easter and on, all the way into Pentecost. To pray the rosary has given me a deeper awareness of Mary's closeness. I have come to pray the rosary in many ways that have brought healing and new life. One of the most effective ways just arose in me spontaneously one day when I was angry and hurt. I began to pray a decade of the rosary, asking Mary to bless the individual with whom I felt in disharmony. Even before I finished the prayer, I found myself wanting to do something pleasant for that person. Now, surely, that had to be Mary's influence! And my response could only be a big smile at my own fears and a prayer of gratitude that we are not alone. Silently praying the rosary while standing in line at the supermarket, while driving the car, while waiting for the pie to come out of the oven has become natural now . . . another source of strength and joy.

My heart has always responded with awe at the word "adoration," even when I had no real sense of what that word meant in a Catholic setting. I discovered that awe is the appropriate response as I sit before the visible consecrated host during contemplative hours of adoration—just being in silence before him. On several occasions while just sitting in the chapel in prayer, I have felt what I can only describe as a beam of love emanating from the tabernacle where the consecrated host rests. I cannot explain it, nor do I need to. I not only accept love's presence in the Eucharist, I accept love's presence wherever and however it comes as gift.

To be Catholic is to be universal—part of a world church. I did not understand this as a definition of the word "catholic" until I began to attend Mass and receive Eucharist wherever I traveled. No matter where, in what language, or with what participants, I am home. The tiny wafer that becomes his body, the sip of wine that becomes his blood unites us. I know without doubt that I am one member in a worldwide family. I can follow the Mass in any language because I know who is present in the breaking of the bread.

So Eucharist becomes each day a mirror of who I am and of whom I am called to become. The heart of my faith as a Catholic is Jesus present in my life, leading me at every moment to become more and more the fullness of whom I am called to be—even through the struggles, stumblings, and sufferings that letting go of my own will sometimes entails. The Eucharist has become my journey—the path and, at the same time, the ever new homecoming. To live Eucharist is to live his life in me and to surrender my life into the mystery of his love.

5

PROTESTANTISM

ROBERT E. KOENIG

"Seek first God's kingdom and God's righteousness!" With words such as these, Jesus initiated what at first was a reform movement within Judaism, but which in time became the worldwide religion known as Christianity. Guided by the example of Jesus, who died on the cross as a result of seeking to do God's will, and inspired by the spiritual power of God unleashed in the resurrection of Jesus, the early Christians resisted the demands of the authorities to conform by declaring, "We must obey God rather than humans" (Acts 5:29).

As the early Christian church became transformed from a persecuted minority to the established religion of the majority, however, it became all too easy for its leaders to identify their own human agendas with the will of God. From time to time, therefore, reformers arose within the church to call it back to what they considered to be its true task. Sometimes the church leaders listened to the voices of reform and the church became renewed—able to minister more effectively to the needs of the times. At other times, the church resisted efforts for change, occasionally with good reason but sometimes unwisely, persecuting those who would call it back to faithfulness.

THE PROTESTANT REFORMATION
During the height of the Middle Ages, the Western branch of the church with headquarters in Rome reigned supreme over the cultural

---

Robert E. Koenig, Ph.D., is an ordained minister in the United Church of Christ. He has worked as editor-in-chief for United Church Press, a publishing house of the United Church of Christ. He is the author of *The Use of the Bible with Adults*, *Jesus Christ: The Basis of Our Faith*, and *Man's Use of God's Power*.

and spiritual life of Europe, playing a decisive role in the political life of the continent. The arts and sciences flourished in what came to be known as the medieval synthesis. Great cathedrals were built with lofty spires pointing the people toward God. Great artists captured the essence of spirituality in sculpture and painting. Theology reigned over science, interpreting all human endeavor from the divine perspective. But as time went on, the very successes of the church tended to draw it away from its fundamental purpose—to witness in word and deed to God's will for the world.

The church, indeed, had fallen on troubled times. In many areas, education of both clergy and laity was neglected. The profound theological insights of the High Middle Ages were beyond the experience of the common people. Worldliness was rampant. Church positions were bought and sold to the highest bidder. The doctrine of forgiveness became converted to a cash transaction for some, so that indulgences—remission from the punishment for sins—could be earned by the performance of secular acts, or purchased by the payment of money. Against these growing abuses, voices were raised in growing number until finally, in the sixteenth century, they culminated in the Protestant Reformation.

Even by the end of the fifteenth century, the church was ripe for reformation; forces unleashed by the church provided the stimulus and fuel for change. External factors wielded their influence as well. In the Renaissance, the resurgence of the arts and sciences brought about a focus on the human earthly condition. Explorers such as Christopher Columbus and Ferdinand Magellan were widening the horizons of the human consciousness. The founding of universities resulted in a new appreciation of the classical languages, which enabled the Bible to be read in its original tongues, Hebrew and Greek, although centuries earlier it had been translated into Latin for regular church services. With the rise of national consciousness came the dissolution of Christendom into independent nation-states. And a resurgence of mysticism, sparked in part by the trauma of the great bubonic plague (the Black Death, which began in Western Europe in 1347), drew many people from the external forms of church life to probe the depths of the inner spiritual life.

Early Reform Movements

As early as 1176, Waldo, a rich merchant of Lyons, responded to the biblical injunction to "sell all that you have and distribute it to the poor, and you will have treasure in heaven; and come, follow me [Jesus]" (Matt. 19:21). Thus began the Waldensian movement, which is still in existence. In the late 1300s John Wycliffe, a biblical scholar at Oxford, began to criticize the existing church structures on the basis of his biblical studies, and eventually began to translate the Bible into English. Wycliffe's teachings spread to Bohemia, where the fiery preacher Jan Hus proclaimed them from the pulpit of the Bethlehem Chapel at the University of Prague. Though Hus was excommunicated and burned at the stake for his beliefs, his followers in Bohemia flourished.

The Beginning of the Reformation

In their protest against the corruption of the church and in their appeal to biblical principles, Wycliffe and Hus were forerunners of the Reformation. The Protestant Reformation actually began on Halloween 1517, when Martin Luther, a young Augustinian monk, tacked on the door of the castle church in Wittenberg ninety-five theses—propositions—that he was willing to debate with all comers. Luther's intent was to call the church back to a biblical understanding of the faith, relying on the authority of the Bible as the word of God.

At first the church authorities tried to debate him, but they were unable to meet his arguments. Finally he was called up before a general council and ordered to recant his position. When he refused, legend has it that he cried out: "I cannot do otherwise. Here I stand. God help me. Amen." By 1526, as a result of his defiant stand and vigorous preaching, a large portion of the church in the German states had broken away from the authority of Rome to follow the teachings of Luther.

Other Reformers

Meanwhile, reformers were at work in other countries. Ulrich Zwingli and John Calvin in Switzerland and John Knox in Scotland sought with varying degrees of success to reform the church in their respective lands, basing their efforts on biblical principles. Henry VIII of England, by an act of Parliament, became head of that country's church—more for political than religious reasons—but his advisors had been impressed by the teachings of Luther and helped to align the Church of England with the Protestant movement.

For some people, however, these efforts to reform the church were not enough. Rejecting the existing structures of the church, including the baptism of infants, these *Anabaptists* (those in opposition to infant baptism) organized new communities of faith based on radical biblical principles, requiring members to be rebaptized on the basis of their confession of faith. During this period in Europe there was no separation of church and state as we know it today. The religion of the ruler usually was the established religion of the country, and other faiths were rarely tolerated. Since the rulers belonged to either Roman Catholic, Lutheran, or Reformed churches, Anabaptists were looked on with suspicion and often were persecuted.

The Reformation in England

A special situation existed in the British Isles, however. When Henry VIII separated the English church from Roman control, the resulting reformation did not go far enough for many people. Some, known as Puritans, tried to purify the church from within. Others, called Independents and, later on, Congregationalists, broke off from the existing parishes and formed new communities of faith—congregations—which governed themselves. The Anabaptists were represented by the Baptist churches, while an even more radical group, the Society of Friends, or Quakers, reacted against forms of worship as well as church structure, preferring to rely on the guidance of the Spirit in their group and individual life.

THE MOVE TO A NEW WORLD

The unique character of Protestantism was not fully established until it migrated to the New World. The North American continent was a haven for groups of devout Christians whose beliefs differed from those of their rulers. Pilgrims and Puritans in Massachusetts, Baptists in Rhode Island, Friends in Pennsylvania were some of the better-known groups that came seeking freedom of worship. The Church of England, of course, was established in all the colonies that were under British rule. In some of the colonies patterns of exclusiveness were brought over from Europe. The Pilgrims and the Puritans in Massachusetts established what at first was a church state in which there was no real distinction between the worshiping congregation and the local government. Later on, as new governors were appointed by the British crown, the Anglican church gained a foothold. In the Virginia colony, however, the Anglican church was established from the beginning.

In several of the colonies freedom of worship was recognized from the beginning. In Pennsylvania, William Penn welcomed not only members of the Society of Friends (Quakers) but people of all persuasions. Many refugees from Germany—Lutheran and Reformed—flocked to this haven. Roger Williams, a Baptist who had been driven from Massachusetts for his beliefs, established freedom of religion in Rhode Island. Lord Baltimore, who obtained the charter for Maryland, established full religious freedom in that colony to provide a refuge for Roman Catholics and others who chafed under the restrictions in England.

Religious Diversity

With the formation of the United States of America, the principle of freedom of religion became established in all the former colonies by the Constitution's Bill of Rights. The flow of immigration increased as people were pushed from their homelands by war, famine, poverty, and political oppression, and pulled by the promise of opportunity and freedom. They brought with them their cultures, which included their religions. They were not just Protestants, but Roman Catholics and Orthodox Christians as well; not just Christians, but Jews, Muslims, Hindus, Buddhists, and a great variety of other Eastern faiths. But at least in the early part of the nineteenth century, the great majority were Protestants from the various countries of Europe. In addition to the different faith communities such as Lutheran, Reformed, Baptist, Anglican, and Quaker, there were the ethnic variations: Swedish, Danish, Norwegian, and German Lutherans; German, Hungarian, French, and Moravian Reformed, to name but a few. Some of these immigrants joined Protestant groups already established, but others brought their own communities with them and exercised their freedom to form a multitude of denominations and sects.

Indigenous Movements

The variety of Protestant groups was not limited to those brought in from other countries. Exercising their newfound freedom, reformers on the North American continent broke away from established groups, seeking to restore the purity of the faith or rebelling against newly developed ecclesiastical structures.

Thus John Wesley and Charles Wesley, for instance, brought from England principles of spirituality and church discipline that resulted in the formation of Methodism. Though the Wesley brothers never left the Church of England, their followers—both in England and in the American colonies—did separate themselves to form a new church. In the early 1800s various groups broke away from the Methodists, Presbyterians, and Baptists in reaction to what they felt to be rigid theological systems and oppressive church organization. Calling themselves "Christian," they tried to return to biblical principles of faith and community organization. In time these churches became parts of other denominations.

The Civil War had a divisive effect upon American Protestantism as well. Denominations with national organizations split between North and South. Thus there were formed the Northern and the Southern Baptists, Methodists, and Presbyterians. Interestingly enough, the Episcopal Church did not split, since the various dioceses looked to the Church of England rather than to a national organization for their unity.

Diversity

It is apparent that the diversity of Protestantism has come from many sources. Theological differences, those grounded on differences of biblical interpretation, were the major original basis for variety, resulting in the Lutheran, Reformed, Baptist, and Quaker traditions. Together with the theological differences there were differences in church organization, which resulted in the hierarchical (Episcopal and Methodist), connectional (Presbyterian), autonomous local church (Congregational and Baptist), and faith community (Friends) structures. As noted above, another major source of diversity was ethnic roots. Toward the middle and later years of the nineteenth century, immigrant Christians from Western Europe were joined by Christians from Russia, the Middle East, and the Far East—the latter group drawn by the obvious lure of America as well as by the great Protestant missionary movement that began early in the century.

The Black Churches

The largest group of ethnic churches, however, came not from immigration or overseas missionary work, but from missionary work among Afro-Americans, most of whom had been brought to the United States as slaves. The earliest black churches, however, were formed by free black Christians in the North, two of the oldest being the African Methodist Episcopal Church, founded in 1816 in Philadelphia, Pennsylvania, and the African Methodist Episcopal Zion Church, founded in 1820 in New York City.

In the South some of the slave-owners permitted or encouraged missionary efforts to convert their slaves to Christianity. After the Civil War a number of black Protestant denominations were formed, reflecting the various denominations of former white slave-owners.

For the most part, the religious style of these denominations was developed during the period of slavery. The message of freedom in the Bible spoke to the deepest needs of those in bondage, offering them hope in this world and in the world to come. Black preachers incorporated the oral skill of storytelling brought over from Africa, and the rhythms of their ancestors were incorporated in spirituals that expressed their deepest feelings.

After the Civil War, blacks were still subject to a century of segregation, but the churches took the lead in the struggle for justice and equal opportunity. During the long years of legalized segregation, the black churches became the arena for the development and exercise of leadership ability. Black ministers were active not only in religious circles, but eventually in politics as well. In the 1950s and 1960s it was the black church that spearheaded the civil rights movement under the leadership of Martin Luther King, Jr. More broadly based efforts continue under the leadership of other black ministers such as Andrew Young and Jesse Jackson.

PRINCIPLES OF THE REFORMATION

Though the Protestant churches are varied in terms of belief, organization, and ethnicity, certain fundamental principles are common to most of them.

The Supremacy of the Bible
over Tradition

In the early Christian church, the authority of both the Bible and oral tradition were equal. By the sixteenth century, however, various practices had arisen that seemed at variance with the findings of new

biblical scholarship. While the reformers were unanimous in assert-
ing the supremacy of the Bible over church tradition, the principle
was applied in two ways. The first, exemplified by the Lutherans, continued most of the traditions that were not at variance with biblical
teaching. The other, more radical approach was to eliminate all practices for which a biblical warrant could not be found.

Beyond this, the way in which the authority of the Bible is understood varies from group to group. Liberal Protestants apply the full
range of historical and literary techniques in biblical interpretation.
Conservatives use sound interpretive methods, but tend to use them
more cautiously. Fundamentalists insist on seven tenets that they
deem fundamental to the Christian faith and which, taken together,
distinguish them from liberal Christians. Some of these tenets are the
insistence on the literal interpretation of Scripture, the miraculous
virgin birth of Jesus, the physical resurrection of Jesus from the dead,
and a devotion to saving missions.

Justification by Faith

This doctrine was at the heart of Luther's protest against the practices
of the church in his day. It holds that salvation comes by God's grace
alone, which is received in faith, not earned by any good work. It
does not deny the importance of good works in the Christian life, but
it holds that good works are a result of faith in God, not a way to earn
God's favor, which is available to all who will receive it in faith.

The Priesthood of
All Believers

First Peter 2:9 succinctly expresses this doctrine:

> But you are a chosen race, a royal priesthood, a holy nation, God's
> own people, that you may declare the wonderful deeds of [the one]
> who called you out of darkness into [God's] marvelous light.

The doctrine was a reaction to the separation of Christians into
clergy and laity, which established the priests thereby as intermedia-
ries between the laity and God. It encouraged direct access to God on
the part of all people. Martin Luther further interpreted it to mean
that each Christian had the responsibility to be a priest to his or her
neighbor, regardless of whether the individual was ordained.

Christian Freedom and
Responsibility

Closely related to the doctrines of the priesthood of all believers and justification by faith is the concept of freedom and responsibility in Christ. Being justified by faith, we are freed from the restrictive demands of the law interpreted in a legalistic fashion, but we are empowered to live a life of responsible service to our neighbor. The law referred to included not only the law of Moses, which was the concern of the apostle Paul, but the canon law of Rome, which circumscribed the freedom of the Christian. In the words of Luther, the Christian is at the same time "a most free person and the humble servant of all."

The seemingly contradictory character of Christian freedom and responsibility is resolved into a true paradox in the concept of the *vocation* or *calling* of a Christian. As Christians, we are called by and empowered by God's spirit to use our God-given abilities in the service of others—not because others make us serve them, but because God guides us into those actions that will meet human need. The concept of vocation has sometimes become narrowed to refer only to the way in which one earns a living: one's job. But it applies to all that we do—in our home and family, in our service to the community, and in our interpersonal relationships, as well as to our particular livelihood.

The Meaning of "Protestant"

In a sense these doctrines are not peculiar to Protestants; rather, they are basic to all Christian belief. In the sixteenth century, however, they represented the areas that the reformers felt were most in need of emphasis if the church was to be renewed.

Crucial to an understanding of the doctrines is the word Protestant as it is applied to a most diverse collection of faith-communities. The word "protest" has two quite different meanings, both of which are necessary to understand the meaning of Protestant. The first meaning is to make a solemn declaration or affirmation, from the Latin *pro,* meaning "for," and *testari,* "to be a witness." The second and more familiar meaning is to register an objection, as in "to protest against."

The word Protestant was used first to refer to those German princes who, at a meeting in 1529, protested *against* an edict that sought to crush the growing reform movement of Martin Luther, and who called *for* the emperor to hold a general council to discuss the situation further. In the course of time the word came to refer to the movement that was protesting *against* the abuses that had crept into the Christian church and that was calling *for* a renewed understanding of the Christian faith based on a return to biblical studies.

CHURCH LIFE

Worship Practices

The center of Protestant church life today is the Sunday morning congregational worship. Sunday, the first day of the week, is also known as the Lord's day, the day on which Jesus rose from the dead. On Sunday, members of the congregation gather to worship God and to learn how to carry out God's will in their lives.

The forms of worship are almost as varied as the number of denominations, but they can be grouped into several types, which vary from the full liturgical order of the Episcopal service to the free, spontaneous meeting of the Friends.

The Episcopal and Lutheran services are adaptations of the Roman Mass, revised to provide a more biblical emphasis, but with chants and congregational responses as well as hymns, a confession of faith, prayers, Scripture lessons from a lectionary, a sermon or homily based on the Scripture, and the recitation of either the Apostles' Creed or the Nicene Creed.

A somewhat simpler version of the full liturgical service, yet one based on the worship practices of the early church during its first three hundred years, has been developed for use in some of the Reformed and Presbyterian churches. A similar type of liturgy with roots in the Episcopal service is used in Methodist churches.

Perhaps the most typical Protestant service of worship, however, is that occurring in the nonliturgical or free churches: a call to worship, hymns, prayers, readings from the Scriptures, a sermon based on the Scriptures, an offering, and a benediction. An interesting variation on this service comes from the great revival movements of the eighteenth and nineteenth centuries on the American frontiers, where, once a year, revivals were held for those who had no other opportunity to worship. The faithful gathered to hear the word and testify to their call. Backsliders from the faith were urged to come forward and repent of their sins. Unbelievers were urged to be converted and to confess their faith. Some churches of denominations such as the Southern Baptists, the Nazarenes, and the Church of God still continue the practice of an altar call following the sermon as a regular part of their Sunday morning worship.

The most unusual form of Protestant worship is the Quaker meeting. At the appointed time, the congregation gathers for silent meditation and the sharing of insights and concerns as guided by the Spirit. Sometimes hymns are sung; sometimes a passage of Scripture is read. A particular problem may have arisen during the week, which someone presents to the whole group for prayerful consideration and action. When the concerns have been heard and considered, the meeting is ended. Not all branches of the Society of Friends worship according to this free pattern, however. In the Midwest, many Quakers follow a standard order of service led by an ordained minister in a simple church building with pews and hymnbooks. But there still is a sense of guidance by the Spirit that continues as one leaves the service of worship to resume one's activities at home and at work.

Basic to all these services—whether the structured liturgy of the Episcopalians or the Spirit-guided meditation of the Friends—is the concept that worship is the response of the people to the goodness and grace of God, in which we acknowledge in awe and wonder, with praise and thanksgiving, God's greatness and love for us. We confess our sins and ask for forgiveness; we hear the instruction concerning God's will for us through the Scriptures and their interpretation. We offer ourselves to God in service to our neighbor as an expression of our thankfulness for all that God has done and continues to do for our welfare. Thus, worship is not just what we do in the Sunday morning service, but is our faithful response to God's grace in our work and play throughout the week. To help them in this task, many people supplement the Sunday morning worship with daily periods of prayer, meditation, and Bible study.

The Sacraments and Rites

A major result of the Protestant Reformation was the reshaping of the Roman Catholic sacramental system. Instead of seven sacraments, the reformers recognized only two as having biblical warrant: baptism and the Lord's Supper, which is also called Holy Communion or the Eucharist. Of the rest, confirmation, marriage, and ordination were recognized as rites of the church; penance was transformed from a private, individual action to a public, corporate action in the confessional prayer of the service of worship. The last sacrament, the rite of absolution, was discontinued.

Baptism. One of the greatest stumbling blocks to unity for Protestants has been the differing conceptions of the conditions for administering the sacrament of Baptism. Some denominations continue the Roman Catholic practice of infant baptism, while others insist on believer's baptism. All denominations recognize three actors in the sacrament: God, the church, and the person being baptized. In performing the act of baptism, usually in the name of the triune God, the church is recognizing God's grace that is offered to all who are willing to accept it and let it transform their lives. The question is, When does it become possible for a person to accept the working of God's grace? Those who insist on believer's baptism say it is when a person is able to confess (profess) faith in God as revealed in Jesus Christ and can commit to a life of love and service in the name of Christ. Those who permit or encourage infant baptism usually acknowledge the validity of believer's baptism but assert that we cannot say when someone has accepted the quality of God's grace. The human response to God's grace and to the witness of the community is a total response, involving more than the intellect. Furthermore, if we are faithful Christians our response to God's grace is not limited to the moment of our baptism but continues throughout our life. Thus, if a person, baptized as an infant, is brought up "in the nurture and admonition of the Lord," he or she can continue to receive and respond to the grace of God to the extent that developing physical, mental, and spiritual capacities allow.

Whether infant baptism or believer's baptism is practiced, however, baptism is a symbolic washing away of sin and reconciliation with God—a dying to sin and rising with Christ—that incorporates one into the body of Christ, the church. For those baptized as believers, this also means joining a local congregation as a responsible participant. Those churches that practice infant baptism usually have another ceremony—confirmation, owning the covenant, or joining the church—by which a person is put on the rolls of the church as an adult member. The rite of confirmation or its equivalent normally is preceded by a period of instruction in the faith, life, and mission of the church that can run anywhere from six weeks to three or more years. (In this, confirmation is similar to the requirements of the Jewish confirmation and to the studies that precede the rites of bar mitzvah and bat mitzvah.)

Conversely, those who practice believer's baptism often have a ceremony of infant dedication, in which parents and congregation pledge to nurture and support the child until he or she reaches an age where a decision in faith is deemed possible.

The Lord's Supper. The reformers were unanimous in rejecting the prevailing Roman Catholic doctrine of transubstantiation in the sacrament of Holy Communion, or the Eucharist. According to this dogma, when the priest raises the bread and the wine and says, "This is my body" or "This is my blood," the elements are transformed spiritually into the body and blood of Jesus Christ, though outwardly their physical characteristics remain unchanged.

In contrast to that doctrine, Luther formulated the doctrine of *consubstantiation,* in which the spirit of Christ is recognized as permeating the elements, being in, with, and under them—*in, mit, und unter.* Zwingli, however, focused on the memorial aspect of the Lord's Supper: "Do this in remembrance of me." For him, the bread and wine were symbols of Jesus' body and blood, though his service did include the invoking of the Holy Spirit to be present.

Whereas baptism is administered once, the Lord's Supper is repeated over and over again. As a remembrance of Jesus' life, death, and resurrection, it is a renewal of the baptismal covenant, an assurance of God's forgiving grace, a strengthening of the bonds of Christian communion one with another, and a giving thanks (eucharist) for God's redeeming love revealed in Jesus Christ. It is at once a solemn and a joyous occasion, standing at the center of the whole Christian worship.

The frequency of the celebration of the Eucharist varies greatly within Protestantism. Some churches celebrate it only three or four times a year—at Christmas or New Year, at Easter, on World Communion Sunday in October, and perhaps on Reformation Sunday. Other churches celebrate it once a month, while still others celebrate it every Sunday as an integral part of morning worship.

Church Education

One outgrowth of the doctrine of the priesthood of all believers has been an emphasis on education. All believers, not just the clergy, were expected to have access to the Scriptures so that they could encounter God's word in its pages and learn what God expected them to do. Wycliffe's translation of the Bible into English and Luther's into German were first steps in helping people to learn about the Christian life. The new services of worship in the language of the people provided opportunities for teaching as the Bible was read and expounded from the pulpit. Catechisms were developed that covered the important teachings of the church in question-and-answer form. Classes to prepare people for confirmation or believer's baptism were formed, and later, with the development of the Sunday school, classes for all ages were offered to provide an ongoing program of Christian education. Though the core of the education program remains the teaching of the Bible, the curriculum has been expanded in many churches to include a study of the history of the church, training in the life of prayer and worship, and exploration of how the church can meet the needs of society today. More recently, an emphasis on people of all ages learning together has been growing.

The Community of Faith

Sunday morning worship and the educational programs of the church have been the main vehicles for maintaining the congregation as a community of faith. Members share experiences, support one another in their joys and sorrows, and prepare for service to the world in the name of Christ. Other programs have been developed within Protestantism that help to maintain a sense of community in a world in which traditional community structures have disappeared. Men's and women's fellowship groups meet separately or together for study and work. Youth groups likewise meet for peer-group support. Intergenerational groups meet not only for educational purposes, but for intergenerational sharing of experiences that goes far to develop a vital community of faith.

HOME AND FAMILY LIFE

In Protestantism the home has traditionally been the foundation on which the local congregation has been built. Within the context of Christian marriage, the home is the place where Christian nurture first begins. Family devotions and Bible reading in a variety of forms still exercise a profound influence on the lives of young and old alike in those homes that employ them. Family celebrations extend the experience of Christian fellowship beyond the weekly services of worship by the congregation.

Marriage as
a Covenant Relationship

Though the marriage ceremony is regarded as a rite rather than a sacrament in Protestantism, the vows that are exchanged are made in the sight of God and are covenantal in nature rather than contractual. In a contract, the relationship is terminated when one partner breaks the contract. In a covenant relationship, the obligations continue whether or not they are upheld. In the marriage ceremony, in the sight of God and the assembled witnesses, the bride and groom pledge to each other their undying love and their intention to care for each other "until death do us part." The officiating minister then declares the fact of their marriage to the assembled company, asks God's blessing on their union, and certifies the fact of their marriage to the state.

This covenantal relationship, in which each cares for the other "in utter unreserve of love," allows for the development of a deepening trust relationship and sharing of experiences that help each partner to grow as a person and to become more sensitive to the needs of the other. In this approach to marriage, the sexual relationship is seen as a God-given opportunity for sharing at the most intimate level possible and as an expression of one's love toward the other physically, mentally, and spiritually. In this covenantal relationship, each partner is regarded as equal to the other in the sight of God. The desired outcome is that each becomes a fuller, more enriched person as the relationship develops and matures.

Unfortunately, the desired outcome is not always forthcoming in some marriages. Sometimes one or both of the marriage partners are unable to engage in the kind of mutual sharing required by the covenantal relationship. When this happens the marriage relationship can turn into a destructive force that hinders the development of each partner—or even threatens to destroy one or both of the partners. In such cases, most Protestant churches recognize that the dissolution of the marriage covenant may be the lesser of two evils and thus necessary, even though a violation of sacred vows.

Christian Nurture

A natural outcome of marriage is the conception, birthing, and raising of children. The concept of responsible parenting includes planning the size of one's family and the spacing of children to allow for the optimum conditions for nurturing the growth and development of each child. Once a child is born, the parents have the opportunity and the responsibility to include the child in the covenantal relationship begun when the parents were married, providing the love and care necessary for the development of human personality in all its dimensions.

In Protestantism, as in other branches of the church and in Judaism, the parents teach trust, values, and faith to the children first by their actions and then by the words that identify and interpret the significance of the actions. Family devotions—including prayer at mealtime, bedtime prayers, the reading of the Bible, and the singing of hymns—along with conversation at mealtimes and family councils provide opportunities to nurture the spiritual life not only of the children but of the parents as well. Needless to say, all the words in the world will do no good unless they reflect the actions and values of the parents. How the parents relate to each other, how they participate in work and community activities, and, especially, how they participate in the life of their faith community are crucial in providing models for Christian faith and action.

The nature of family life has undergone great changes during the past hundred years. At one time the extended family was the norm. Children had not only their parents but uncles, aunts, grandparents, and cousins with whom they interacted and from whom they learned. As society became more mobile, the extended family gave way to the nuclear family, consisting of parents and children, with only an occasional coming together of the larger family at special times. Today, as with other faiths, a minority of Protestant Christians live in nuclear families. The rest live as single-parent families, childless couples, or single adults. For these people, as well as for nuclear and extended families, the local church can be a larger family, providing spiritual nourishment and companionship that helps each person grow to the fullest of his or her capabilities.

CHURCH AND SOCIETY

The relationship of the Protestant churches to society has been a checkered one. In Lutheran countries, the state was seen as ordained by God to keep law and order in society, leaving the church to minister to the spiritual needs of the people. In Reformed territory, church and state were more closely linked. Both John Calvin and Ulrich Zwingli exerted profound influence on the promulgation of laws and the conduct of government. In England, the Anglican church was the established church, while the Independents, Baptists, Quakers, and Roman Catholics were independent of government control.

Separation of Church and State

Early Protestants accepted the principle that the religion of the ruler was the religion of the state, and in America the principle of the established church was initially perpetuated in many of the colonies. However, numerous forms of Protestantism, bitter experiences with established churches, plus the presence of Roman Catholic and Jewish communities were instrumental in the creation of a secular nation. The First Amendment of the United States Constitution declares, "Congress shall make no law respecting an establishment of religion, or prohibiting the free exercise thereof." Clearly, this does not derive from, much less is it, Reformation doctrine.

Since the late eighteenth century, Protestants have generally accepted the principle of freedom of religion in the amendment as consonant with their theological stance, although with significant differences in interpretation. For some this means that church groups should be concerned only with spiritual matters and should avoid economic or political concerns. Others, who hold that all aspects of life have a spiritual dimension, feel that Christians have a responsibility to play an active role in the shaping of political decisions that affect the basic structures of society. In the past, these differing interpretations helped to distinguish liberal Protestants from most fundamentalists and many conservatives, with the liberals being most active on the political scene. Now, however, all branches of Protestantism are beginning to recognize the importance of influencing legislation in favor of particular moral stances. Some fundamentalists groups, though, have gone even further, attempting to influence not only legislation but the essential freedom of belief. Concomitant with matters purely of their religious interpretation have been attempts to control education through censorship and to deny other groups and minorities the right of free religious choices. In the process they have also, incidentally, succeeded in amassing large fortunes and vast properties. Here, specifically, we must recognize the highly organized evangelical sects that are led by a number of "charismatic" televangelists, some of whom have even ventured into the political arena, as seen in the 1988 presidential primaries.

At Work in the World

Regardless of how Protestants interpret the concept of the separation of church and state, most would agree that one's daily life should reflect the faith professed in worship on the Lord's day. As a well-known motto placed on the door of many churches proclaims: "Enter to worship; depart to serve." Thus one is called to live out one's faith at home, at work, and at play—at all times. The need to live out one's faith applies to the Christian community as well as to individual Christians. Thus Protestant churches have established hospitals to care for the mentally and physically ill, homes to care for the homeless, food centers to feed the hungry, and schools to nurture the mind. They have witnessed against social evils such as slavery, economic and racial injustice, and the denial of human rights. Some have taken an active part in the political process, working for the repeal of unjust laws or the passage of legislation for a more humane and just society.

The Missionary Movement

All branches of Protestantism subscribe to one form of interaction between church and society—the response to Jesus' command to "make disciples of all nations" (Matt. 28:19). But here again, the command has been interpreted in various ways. For some, the command means only proclaiming the good news of salvation by faith in Jesus Christ, and teaching the ways of Christianity. For others, it has meant showing forth the love of God in Christ by deed as well as by word, establishing hospitals and schools, giving help in agricultural, industrial, and scientific fields so that persons may be helped to develop to their full potential. But whatever the form, the imperative to spread the gospel continues to be acknowledged by most Protestants. An example of most zealous activity in spreading the gospel, particularly by personal canvassing, is that of the Jehovah's Witnesses.

The Ecumenical Movement

One of the most significant results of the missionary movement in the nineteenth and twentieth centuries has been the rise of the ecumenical movement. The Reformation led to the splintering of the Christian church into many competing groups. The twentieth-century ecumenical movement is working to bring churches together in cooperation and end competition so that the witness of the gospel to the world will have a greater impact. At one time European and North American missionaries in non-Christian countries would establish their own particular versions of Christianity, perpetuating the divisions that existed in their homelands. Today, however, the historical bases for these divisions are for the most part meaningless. Inspired by biblical calls for unity in the name of Christ, churches have begun to challenge the existing denominational and sectarian structures, bringing about the birth of ecumenism.

More recently, the Orthodox churches have joined the movement; after the Second Vatican Council, the Roman Catholic church began to seek closer relations with the "separated churches." Though organic reunion between Protestant, Roman Catholic, and Orthodox churches—or even among Protestant churches themselves—does not seem likely in the foreseeable future, the move toward spiritual unity is gaining momentum. There are growing efforts to find common ground in faith, and when practical the churches do work together to implement joint solutions. Meanwhile, the unique contributions of the Protestant, Orthodox, and Roman Catholic churches enrich the life of all, thus providing bridges of understanding and reconciliation.

6

WHY I AM
A PROTESTANT

JEAN H. MORTON

First and foremost, I believe in God. After more than fifty years of living, I know God is. This has become the inescapable bedrock of my life. Like Carl Jung who, when queried by a reporter, said, "I do not believe, I know that God is," I also answer, God is. Faith in God is an ongoing journey. It is a permanent thread woven into the unfolding fabric of my life. Ever since a numinous experience in college, I have known God is. Understanding this reality since then has involved a panorama of human experience. My faith consists of both intellectual and experiential knowledge. My faith journey has included times of doubt and questioning as well as of deep sureness. God has sustained me in times of great joy and deep grief. I have come to know, with the psalmist, that there is indeed no night so dark, nor depth so deep that I am separated from the love of God.

Second, my faith and beliefs about God are Christian. I believe that in a unique and mysterious way God chose to communicate to all humanity through the specific life and teachings of Jesus of Nazareth. Jesus' life, ministry, and teaching are historical realities. Jesus' resurrection as the Christ is a matter of faith, attested to by millions of believers in every generation. The living Christ is encountered with life-changing impact by individuals in every generation. This encounter has changed my life. Christ has become the center of my life, impacting all that I do. The more that I come to know Christ within my

Jean H. Morton is an ordained Presbyterian minister. She received her M.Div. degree from New York Theological Seminary in 1988. Her essay was written prior to her ordination, when she was an ordained elder.

heart, the more this becomes the growing reality of my life. A metaphor I like to use to express my understanding of this is to say that Christ's life and teaching is like a perfect multifaceted crystal, through which each generation catches a partial glimpse of God's truth, love, wisdom, and justice. Each generation must interpret and apply God's truths to its particular time and place.

Finally, I am a Protestant and, more specifically, a Presbyterian. I believe that the Bible is the Word of God. My study and understanding of the Scriptures lead me to theological beliefs that only allow me to be a Protestant. We live in a day when it is tempting and popular to blur and mix ideas from different faiths. I believe that if all the monotheistic faiths are to understand and respect each other, it is important to be clear about our differences. Understanding can only be built on clarity about that which is distinctive to our beliefs. It is for this reason that I have agreed to write this essay about some of the distinctive Presbyterian beliefs that are important to my particular journey of faith. If the Protestant faith is an ongoing active part of a person's life, that person is not just generally Protestant. An individual Protestant believer is an active member of a specific faith community that is usually related to a specific denomination. My Presbyterian tradition is a part of the Reformed tradition of Protestantism. As such, I believe that being a part of a community of believers is an integral part of living out one's faith. This means that as a Presbyterian I am expected to participate in the life of the congregation. Baptisms are community events, not private. The entire community accepts responsibility for the new member. Protestantism is formed by several streams of tradition. It was the "reformers" and the Reformed tradition that initially shaped Protestantism.

There are four basic principles that have become very important to my understandings of Christianity. They have been formative to the way I live out my faith in Jesus Christ as the Son of God. These four principles are basic to Reformed Protestant Christianity. They are (1) the primacy of Scripture and the Holy Spirit; (2) justification by faith; (3) the priesthood of all believers; and (4) unity within diversity.

The Protestant reformers believed that the Bible is the sole authority for the Christian faith. It is the Word of God. The Holy Spirit attests to the Scriptures through inward illumination. It is through the Holy Spirit that the Bible is understood. These two beliefs, which inform each other, were basic to the beginning of the Protestant Reformation. They are still basic to Protestant Christianity as distinct from Catholic Christianity. In addition, Presbyterians then and now affirm that "God alone is Lord of the conscience."

Luther and Calvin believed in "justification by faith." This doctrine basically says that it is by faith alone and the grace of God that a person is saved. What is required of an individual is a quality of the heart which characterizes that person's relationship to God through prayer. Only God in Christ can save. Works and ritualistic ceremonies do not bring salvation. Works are the result of a grateful heart. "Works" or deeds are done out of gratitude to God, and indeed will be done, but it is faith alone that saves. The two doctrines of *"sola scriptura"* and "justification by faith" launched the Protestant Reformation and changed the face of history.

The doctrine of the "priesthood of all believers" is very important to me. It is basic to my understanding of who I am in relationship to God, and how I live out my faith in the structure of the church. It is also a very basic doctrine of Reformed theology. It says that all people who are baptized and who have professed their faith are members of the church and are responsible for witnessing to their beliefs to others. Each believer has a personal relationship with God through Christ and the Holy Spirit. Each believing Christian is called upon to witness to his or her faith by word and deed. Calvin believed that every person's vocation was to be done for the glory of God. A Christian's secular "work" could be sacred when devoted to God. The call to live out one's faith is not separate from the rest of life.

The Presbyterian church has made the doctrine of the "priesthood of all believers" so basic that it has sought to live it out faithfully in the very form of its church governance. The Presbyterian church is governed by a representative system based on the presbytery, a specific geographic unit made up of the churches within that area. All Presbyterian ministers serving in that geographic area, whether in the parish or in other ministries, are members of the presbytery, not of the church they serve if a parish minister. An equal number of elders are chosen from the churches to be commissioners to presbytery. Together they constitute the presbytery, which is the governing body above the local church. Lay commissioners are elders, ordained by their local church. Each local congregation is governed by a body of elders, called the session. Although ordained as an elder for life, each elder serves for a three-year term and may only be reelected for a second consecutive term, although they may serve again at a later date. Each presbytery elects at least one minister commissioner and one elder commissioner to represent them at synod, a regional area. Each presbytery also elects at least one other elder commissioner and one other minister commissioner to represent them at the national meeting of the General Assembly. Additional commissioners are sent in accord with the number of churches in the particular presbytery. Synods and the General Assembly are responsible for missions and other tasks that no one church or presbytery could do alone. Each body is a deliberative body. It is understood that each commissioner is to vote according to his or her own conscience and the leading of the Holy Spirit. Commissioners cannot be instructed how to vote. Each General Assembly (or synod) meeting in a particular year speaks by consensus for that particular General Assembly (or synod), although some ongoing commitments and positions are supported from year to year. It is very important to understand that no one person ever speaks for the entire Presbyterian church by virtue of office. The power is in the deliberative body as a whole. The structure by which the Presbyterian church seeks to be faithful in its witness is an important living-out of our relationship to God and how we understand ourselves to be a servant people. It concretizes our belief in the doctrine of the priesthood of all believers.

As a student of political science, I value the theoretical understanding of the representative presbyterian system. Hands-on experience has confirmed for me its value as a system of governance. I have been a commissioner to my presbytery. The presbytery has elected me, once, to serve as a commissioner to General Assembly, and three times as a commissioner to our synod. Each term is for that one time. I have also been elected to serve a three-year term on the synod's Ministries Agency, an ongoing working committee of the synod. As with all systems, presbyterian governance is dependent on the very human people within it. My experiences of serving the church have taught me that when used as intended, it is a system that works very well. The Holy Spirit does inform its deliberations and work.

My experiences of serving the presbytery, synod, and General Assembly as an ordained elder have taught me the great workable value of the concept of "unity within diversity," which is the third concept that I have chosen to write about as important to me. Because no one person speaks authoritatively for the Presbyterian church, this is an important principle. Its formulation goes back to the earliest days of Presbyterianism in the United States. There were three different strands of Presbyterianism at this time, each with slightly different ideas about their faith. Recognizing that the unity of their Reformed Christian faith was far greater than their differences, they developed the concept of "unity within diversity." It has served the church well. The first time that I was a commissioner to the Synod of the Northeast, I experienced the loving genius of this concept. Within a working subcommittee, diametrically opposed viewpoints were presented and discussed. A recommendation supported by the majority was worked out and brought before the entire committee. Here it was further discussed, amended, and finally approved for presentation to the entire synod body, where it was again open for debate, amendment, and final approval or disapproval. Through this experience, I learned that people of opposite opinions can still appreciate and care for each other as Christians. It is a lesson I have never forgotten. The challenge of finding unity within diversity is one our entire world must learn. We must learn how to live with each other with all our diversity, or none of us will survive in this nuclear age.

The fourth concept that is distinctive to the Presbyterian church and other Reformed churches is that as a church we are both reformed and always reforming. In a sense this is an important corollary to all that I have written about the presbyterian system. We are a Reformed Protestant Christian church. However, as times change and new situations arise, the church goes on reforming in each generation under the guidance of the Holy Spirit. We live in ongoing dialogue with the Bible, the guidance of the Holy Spirit, and God as we seek to live out our faith in our daily lives as a church and God's people.

As a woman, no essay about what my faith and my church mean to me would be complete without some expression of gratitude for the Presbyterian church's clear affirmation of the equality of women and men before God. As with all justice issues, progress is at times slow, but there is indeed progress. The church has been ordaining women, as well as men, to the office of elder for almost sixty years. Women have been ordained as ministers of the word (clergy) for more than thirty years. Not only has this equality been endorsed as a part of our polity, but units of justice for women are actively working throughout the church to raise consciousness and ensure the modeling of this equality.

United Presbyterian Women is an organization that has had a major impact on my faith journey. It is an autonomous organization with full voice and vote at each judicatory (governing body) level. Its members have been responsible for their own programming, missions, and budget. Since its earliest beginnings in missionary societies, United Presbyterian Women has been concerned about people's needs and finding ways to meet these needs through missions and Christian education. Leadership development and issues of justice, both here and throughout the world, are other areas of strong concern. United Presbyterian Women has a structure which parallels that of the church, starting with local associations, then moving out into wider areas with presbyterials, synodicals, and the national organization of United Presbyterian Women. I will never forget my first national triennium meeting in 1976. The theme for the meeting was "Live into Hope." This theme was based on two scriptural passages in the gospel of Luke: "Mary's Song," and the following words that Jesus read from Isaiah in the synagogue in Nazareth on the sabbath: "The Spirit of the Lord is upon me, because he has chosen me to bring good news to the poor. He has sent me to proclaim liberty to the captives and recovering of sight to the blind, to set free the oppressed and announce that the time has come when the Lord will save his people" (Luke 4:18–19, TEV). Jesus proclaimed that with this reading of these words from Isaiah, they had been fulfilled. This scripture passage is very important to my understanding of who Jesus is and who we are called to be. They are an integral part of my understanding of both the Christian faith and of who I myself am called to be. To love God is to do justice. The Presbyterian church has often affirmed this in all areas of social justice. The meeting's theme, "Live into Hope," had a deep impact on my life. It was both challenging and inspirational. Many worldwide issues of injustice were addressed, and we were called to make responsible decisions about them. Moreover, each one of us was challenged to break whatever chains personally bound us—chains of fear or guilt, for example—and to move toward greater wholeness in the assurance of Christ's love for us. This is ever God's call, today and for tomorrow. The logo for the national meeting was a line drawing of four women in four positions, progressing from the prone to standing tall and praising God, a visual image I treasure.

Since that time my faith has continued to be challenged, stretched, and deepened in a variety of ways. I have grown intellectually, psychologically, and spiritually. United Presbyterian Women and other church programs, as well as my own study and reading, have been strong components of my growth. They have widened my horizons and given me deeper understanding.

The events of my life and a deepened spiritual walk of prayer and faith have been of equal importance. My eldest son was killed at the age of twenty-five by a car out of control, which hit him while he was standing on the curb. Seven years after this, and quite recently, my husband died unexpectedly of a heart attack. I have indeed come to know the preciousness of life. I know that there is no depth so dark that God is not there. I have learned that my faith is the bedrock of my life, and that it is far stronger than I ever dreamed. Shortly after my son's death I wrote a poem, which I offer now as my gift of hope and faith. Twice in my life new life has come again after deepest tragedy and despair.

WINTER OF THE SOUL

My life is a barren wasteland,
Devoid of anyone to laugh, to cry, to share with.
Life's blizzards have blotted out
And swept away all familiar paths.

There is no new trail left to try,
Only uncharted, guideless wasteland,
Like the snowswept land, outside my window.

I stand like the gray weathered, leafless tree,
Rooted to one spot, stubbornly still standing.
Some stubborn, faint flame of life,
Still rooted in faith,
Won't let me give up.

Deep in the innermost reaches of my soul
A still, small voice says: God is,
Withstand, wait.
A time will come when sap will rise,
Leaves will once again sprout from lifeless branches.

As long as the taproot holds,
Clings to the soil of faith
And the tree still stands,
There is hope for new life in some distant spring.

Winds may break
And tear away whole limbs,
But as long as the tree stands
There is time for a new season.

Indeed, I did learn that, in spite of grief, there comes a time for a new season and for new life. Faith in God is the bedrock for new beginnings, and for creative new possibilities. The power of God touches our lives even in the midst of darkness and empowers us.

It is my personal hope that as each one of us is drawn closer to God in deepened faith, the one creator God who is within all and through all and who inspires us all will enable us to begin to build bridges of understanding to each other. For fifteen years I participated in a community interfaith dialogue meeting among two Protestant churches (Presbyterian and Episcopalian), two Catholic churches, and two congregations of Jewish faith, a Reform temple and a Conservative synagogue. More recently I traveled to the Holy Land and also to ancient biblical sites in Greece and Turkey. Through these experiences my understanding and appreciation of the monotheistic faiths has been deepened. God is the great creative heart of us all and of all the universe. If our world is to survive as we know it, all of us must attempt to build bridges between our diverse faiths, bridges that connect through respect of each other and not uniformity.

The Spirit of God seems to be moving in new ways throughout the world today. Barriers between peoples are being broken down, one after another. It is my deep conviction that God's hand is moving in the movements around the world that are replacing centuries-old concepts of the subservience of women, with new concepts of equal partnership alongside men. The Presbyterian church has played a major role in kindling my dream for equality, justice, increased freedom, and new possibilities for all women. The world will benefit from the skills and talents women have to contribute. This concluding poem was written as an expression of my new vision for all women. It is also expressive of a wider vision of a world wherein all peoples work toward justice and respect, moving increasingly toward the biblical vision of shalom.

RAINBOW FOOTSTEPS

Rainbow footsteps beyond the wilderness,
Brush strokes in time.
Pearls strung on an incomplete necklace.

Slowly, into, then out of the wilderness we move,
One faltering step, then another,
Informed by the opposites.
Informed by the deeply feminine.

Challenged, by the ever searching word of God,
Blowing where it will.
Informed most of all by the flickering light of paradox.
Offering in symbol and question
The answer somehow dimly perceived.

Deep in the depths of my heart's soul,
Image of a crystal clear fountain.
Diamond drops caught by the light,
Sparkling in myriad rainbows of shalom.

Offering renewal for all my wearied, defeated nights.
Inner calm for outward tempest.
One woman's Holy Grail—symbol of Thou.

Thou who in paradox is beyond all creation.
Yet, in the smallest beating heart of it.
Holding all, encompassing all in a rainbow circle.

7

ISLAM

INTRODUCTION

"There is no God but God, and Muhammad—Peace be upon him—is His Messenger!" With this daily invocation, Muslims in Indonesia and Iran, Paris and Chicago proclaim the essence of Islam: God's unity and Muhammad's prophethood. Bound by the prescribed religious use of the Arabic language, in which the Qur'an is written, a common liturgical calendar, and the daily proclamation of God's oneness and Muhammad's message, Muslim people the world over appear united.

Many will, however, acknowledge that things are not as they appear. The existence of past and present disunity, both religious and political, has plagued the Islamic community. There have been attempts over the past eighty years to bridge the divisions within Islam and to heal the disunity within Islamic societies. These efforts have succeeded in part in reviving and renewing traditional Islamic values and the Islamic community's self-esteem. These efforts at Islamic ecumenism (the movement to bring harmony and unity among the sects), so much a part of Protestant and Catholic discussions for the past century, are not well known. At the same time, a new kind of chauvinism called by some "revivalism" or "fundamentalism," and by others "religious nationalism," is evident in certain Muslim com-

Thomas M. Ricks, Ph.D., is Director of the Office of International Studies, Assistant Director of the Center for Contemporary Arab and Islamic Studies, and Adjunct Professor of History at Villanova University. He has written extensively on the history of Iran and the Middle East.

munities and has been the rationale for much of the violence that continues today.

For most people in the West, Islam and Muslims are mysterious. Despite the recent media coverage of the Iranian Revolution, the Great Mosque takeover in 1979, or the recurrent Shi'ite militancy in Lebanon, the Islamic faith remains foreign and strange to many people, even though, of the almost 900 million Muslims living and working in the world, many are in familiar places like New York City, Paris, or Beijing. For most Western observers Islam is a tangle of myths, restrictions, and "backward" prohibitions associated with Saracens, fanaticism, and terror. Muslims, often clothed in flowing gowns or masked in black veils, remain puzzling at best. Consequently, though much about Islam has been printed in newspapers and reported on newscasts, the movement toward understanding Islam has just begun.

It is important to mention the Judaic and Christian roots of Islam, for the ancient links between Judaism, Christianity, and Islam are well documented. Moses, Abraham, and Jesus are not only deeply respected by Muslims as prophets, they are also continually mentioned in Islamic texts, beginning with the Qur'an (Koran) itself, and are an integral part of Islam's growth. Moses, Abraham, and Jesus themselves, as well as God's messages that each brought to humankind, are sacred and precious to the Islamic peoples. To Muslims, though, the prophethood of Muhammad and his message, coming after those of Moses, Abraham, and Jesus, is an extension of the previous messages from God and a summing up of those messages. Thus, Muhammad's message is the fulfillment of all those that preceded it, and Muhammad himself is the "signet" (seal) in the ring of prophecy and closes the prophetic cycle begun by Moses. By Muslims, his is considered the best testament of them all: he continues the Old and the New Testaments and synthesizes them into the Qur'an.

Muslims

Today Islam (literally, "submission to God's message") is the religious belief of those in Muslim communities throughout the world. Muslims ("those who submit") live and work in fields and factories, workshops and supermarkets, offices and classrooms. Although committed to their own religious observances (that is, to the Pillars of

Islam), Muslim men or women differ little from their neighbors, particularly their Jewish or Christian neighbors whose prophetic heritage they have shared so intimately. Each year Christians, in preparation for Easter, fast in observance of Lent. The Muslim world fasts for thirty days in preparation for *'Id al-Fitr,* the festival ceremonies ending the ninth month of the Islamic calendar, Ramadan. Like Jews and Christians, Muslims look to Jerusalem as a holy city and a pilgrimage center. Jerusalem is the site of Muhammad's ascension to Heaven and also the first of the Islamic holy cities. In remarkably similar ways, Judaism and Islam share many dietary laws, inheritance practices, liturgical seasons, and festivals.

Unlike Judaism or Christianity, however, or Zoroastrianism (the other ancient religion of the Middle East), Islam has no prescribed clerical hierarchy or priesthood. All Muslims are brothers and sisters alike, distinguished primarily by scholarship, sanctity, and age. Islam demands a sense of balance within the individual and sharing in the life of the community, whether the person be a follower or a leader. Thus, decisions are usually made by a council through consensus, in a way similar to that of certain Protestant groups in the post-Reformation era. The Muslim of today, then, is anyone who is prepared to submit to the concept of God's oneness and to the message of Muhammad.

The trappings or symbols of Islam clearly have their origins in the Middle East, more specifically in the societies and cultures of the Arabian peninsula. Regardless of how such symbols or concepts are modified within other cultures, Islam is without doubt an integral part of the past and present worlds of Middle Eastern peoples, whether they be Persian, Turkish, Kurdish, or Arabic-speaking, or whether they be Jewish or Christian. As much as Moses was a part of the history of Egypt and Jesus a part of Palestine, so Muhammad was part of the society and politics of pre-Islamic Arabia. In many ways, knowing the origins of Islam will clarify much that is presently misunderstood about Islam.

HISTORY

Pre-Islamic Arabia

Before the birth of Muhammad and Islam, Judaism and Christianity had long been part of the commercial, religious, and cultural life of

Mecca, Medina, and other market centers of Arabia. Jewish and Christian merchants and travelers resided in or traveled to such places. Pre-Islamic Arabia was the southern terminus for trade routes from the eastern Mediterranean coastal towns and remote market centers, from towns and cities such as Alexandria, Egypt; Jaffa, Palestine; Antioch and Damascus, Syria; and the towns and centers of the Mesopotamian Valley (now Iraq).

In addition, Jewish, Christian, and Arab tribes and merchants lived and worked in the smaller towns of western Arabia. But there was more to pre-Islamic Arabia than just towns and merchants; rural, isolated village, nomadic, and seminomadic peoples were also a part of the polytheistic pre-Islamic world of Arabia.

The nomadic people utilized the vast rangelands and oases of the Arabian highlands, moving from place to place for food and water for their herds. In central Arabia, except for the occasional trading town that linked the Persian Gulf and eastern Arabian coast with the central plains and western Arabian trade routes, only oases and scattered villages were common. In the Arabian world, markets and shrines were linked. The herdsmen, like the coastal and highland villagers, visited the larger towns both to trade and for religious meetings. Merchants and priests, or shrine keepers, worked toward the same goals: the growth of the markets and the expansion of the shrines. This dual growth would benefit each group during the annual religious pilgrimage and market-fair season.

Mecca was the most important commercial and religious center of the Arabian Peninsula, for it was here that one could visit the Ka'ba, as well as a number of other shrines. Embedded in the cubic structure of the Ka'ba was a black stone said to have been brought to Abraham by Angel Gabriel, now believed to be part of a meteorite. The Ka'ba had long been one of the main attractions during the annual ten-day pilgrimage and fair in Mecca. As the pilgrims arrived, they would don seamless white garments, walk seven times around the Ka'ba, pray at Mt. Arafat, and sacrifice a sheep on the tenth day. The pre-Islamic pilgrims sought out shopkeepers, listened to poetry, bartered goods brought from their towns, villages, or pastoral camps, and took part in games and contests. In time, the poetry recitations, the athletic contests that included horse and camel racing, and the goods bartered during the Mecca pilgrimage made that town the economic and cultural center of the peninsula.

The dominant merchant clan in Mecca, known as the Quraysh, controlled most trade, secured the caravan routes, protected the Ka'ba and other shrines, and dominated the cultural and political affairs of the merchant town. The Quraysh grew to know both the Jewish and Christian merchants and travelers who moved about in the Fertile Crescent along the eastern end of the Mediterranean and in other parts of Arabia, and the pastoral and peasant leaders of the western Arabian region. It was not surprising to find, therefore, among the various gods at the shrines in Mecca, the god named Allah (in Arabic) who was the same as El-loh and Elohim of the Old Testament. In Mecca itself there was a small group of people known as the *hanif* who appear to have monotheistic beliefs. These influences played a critical role not only in Muhammad's youth but also in the formation of Islamic practices—practices linked to monotheism, the annual pilgrimage, the caliphate (the successors of Muhammad as leader of Islam), the importance of Jerusalem, and the role of trade and merchants in the development of Islam and Islamic societies.

Muhammad, the Prophet of God

In 570 C.E., Muhammad was born in Mecca, a member of the elite Quraysh tribe. He spent his youth in his grandfather's household, since his parents had died when he was very young. He grew up in the commercial and religious shadow of Mecca, the great merchant town, hearing not only the sounds of the bustling metropolitan trading center but also the dissension of interfamily feuding. At the beginning of the seventh century Mecca was a prosperous town for some but others were poor artisans, caravaneers, or slave laborers. The sharp contrast in social and political power among these groups did not escape the attention of the young Muhammad.

At age twenty-four Muhammad was employed by a wealthy, older merchant woman, Khadija, whose goods were traded as far north as Damascus. While supervising her commercial affairs, Muhammad traveled north to trade in the markets of Jerusalem and Damascus. Among his travel companions were Jews and Christians; possibly the Judeo-Christian roots of Islam began in those days. Muhammad became known as an honest and knowledgeable merchant and soon married Khadija, thereby quickly becoming influential in Mecca and in the Quraysh tribe.

In 610, at age forty, Muhammad, as was custom, retired to a nearby cave to meditate during Ramadan, the traditional month of fasting. While in meditation, he heard a voice command him: "Read in the name of the Lord who created, created man of a blood clot. . . ." Frightened, Muhammad related his experience to Khadija, who in turn repeated the story to her Christian cousin, Waraqah ibn Nawfal, a *hanif.* The cousin is reported to have said, "And lo, he will be a prophet to this people. Bid him to be of a good heart." This momentous occasion on which Muhammad first heard the call of Angel Gabriel is commemorated in Islam as the Night of Power. Important to all Muslims, it is celebrated on the twenty-seventh day of Ramadan.

Later, Muhammad again heard Angel Gabriel, who now bid him: "Arise and warn." Muhammad knew at this point that he had been chosen as God's prophet, and he received more frequent calls while in the cave. For the next ten years, Muhammad preached the unity of God in the streets of Mecca, stating:

> Say: He is Allah, the One!
> Allah, the eternally Besought of All!
> He begetteth not nor was begotten
> And there is none comparable unto Him.
> (Qur'an, 112)

In the Judeo-Christian tradition of prophethood, and as the final prophet, Muhammad frequently reaffirmed the messages of Moses, Abraham, and Jesus and spoke of Adam, Noah, Jonah, and Mary. In doing so, he condemned idolatry and preached the unity of God who had power over life. His message was simple: There is only one God. Forget the many gods of Mecca. The one God is both compassionate and merciful and is the God of all people, Jewish, Christian, and even those who do not yet believe. This God is also the God of the Arab people, who call Him Allah. Muhammad emphasized in those early years the importance of God's message for the people of the Arabian Peninsula, and the punishment awaiting those who, on their pilgrimage, came to Mecca to worship the many gods at other shrines. There was to be only one shrine in veneration of the one God and only one message to the Arab people.

Initially Muhammad had few followers. His wife, his cousin Ali, and his servant Zayd were among the first. Abu Bakr, a prominent member of the Quraysh, was one of the few men of status who accepted Muhammad's message; the majority of Meccans either ignored him or scorned his beliefs, preferring to believe that he was possessed or mad. For many Meccans, Muhammad's message presented a dilemma. While he was one of them and a member of the leading Qurayash family, his condemnation of idolatry and his impassioned plea for a religious community of all people regardless of blood bonds troubled them. While he knew what the impact of his message would be on the Meccan merchant community and on their investments in the shrines and fairs of Mecca, Muhammad did not refrain from preaching. Rather, as the years passed, he increased his religious activism. For the rest of his life the revelations given to Muhammad continued. In their written form they became known as the Qur'an, or reading.

In 619 Muhammad faced his greatest setback: both his beloved Khadija and his grandfather and longtime protector died. Soon he began to receive threats of violence and possible persecution. Responding to an invitation from the people of the neighboring town of Yathrib to arbitrate a dispute between two warring tribes, Muhammad left Mecca. And, in 622, he and his followers permanently moved to the safety of Yathrib, where they were made welcome. Not long after, Yathrib was renamed Medina, or the "City of the Prophet." The year 622 became known as the "Year of the Emigration" (*hijra* or "hegira") and marks the beginning of the Islamic calendar (year one).

Sunni and Shi'i Islam

In 632 C.E. the Prophet Muhammad died in Medina. During the last years of his life there had evolved around him an oral body of rules regarding conduct and behavior based on the Qur'an and on his sayings and practices. Collectively, those rules and the additions made by the *hadiths* (accounts of what Muhammad said, did, and permitted) are known as the Sunna. Today, the majority of Muslims are Sunni Muslims, so called because they follow the principles of the Qur'an, the traditions (*hadiths*), and the model of the Prophet's life.

Over the next three hundred years (632–932), challenges to the interpretations of the Sunna grew as the Islamic world expanded, first into the Fertile Crescent and Iran, and then westward through North Africa into Spain and east into central Asia and to the Ganges Valley of northern India. The various societies, languages, customs, ways of survival, and laws of these new Muslim peoples and lands accounted for many of the differences of opinion that emerged about the Sunna. And the intense struggles between the Meccan and Medinan families for the leadership of the Islamic community (and eventual empire) created new practices and rules for the early Islamic peoples. The earliest and greatest challenge to the new Islamic community was the emergence of the Shi'i, or partisans of the Caliph Ali.

Between 632 and 661, four of the Prophet's closest followers and relatives were chosen in turn as caliphs, successors to the Prophet. The first three distinguished themselves as skillful political and military leaders. The fourth caliphate, that of Ali (d. 661), produced a split within the Islamic community that survives to this day. Claiming that the first three caliphs were usurpers of Ali's claim to the community's leadership, the Shi'i argued that Ali was the most righteous and best example of the Prophet's life. Several hundred years later, the political and legal claim was transformed into a religious and social concept: the just Ali embodies the "spirit" and "light" of the Prophet. Thus, the Shi'i, while accepting the basic pillars (doctrines) of Islam added several of their own: (1) the Doctrine of the Imamate (caliphate), or spiritual embodiment of the Prophet through Ali and his offspring; (2) the Doctrine of the Return of the Hidden Imam (or caliph), a belief in the "second coming" of a hidden, previously unrecognized Imam who would restore justice and equality to humankind and perpetuate the true caliphate; (3) the Doctrine of Interpretation (*ijtihad*); and (4) the Doctrine of Imitation (*taqlid*). The last three concepts, so much a part of Shi'ite political and religious theory, allowed for continuous and innovative interpretations of the Sunna and an obligatory attachment to a spiritual leader. The Imam referred to here is not the same imam who leads prayers in a mosque but the divinely inspired heir to the political and religious leadership of the Shi'ites.

After the split between the Sunnis and Shi'ites, the caliphate was split between two warring political dynasties, the Umayyads and the Abbasids. A caliphate existed until as late as 1924, but its powers were seized early on by factions and people representing temporal powers only rather than the whole of Islam.

With the problem of succession to the Prophet's leadership came the problem of the rules and regulations that were closely tied to the customs and traditions of western Arabia but not to those of the Fertile Crescent, North Africa, Iran, or India. Between 632 and 932, much had changed within the Islamic societies due to numerous conquests, political and social changes in Europe and Asia, changes in land and water usage brought about by troop movements and colonization, and the sheer size of the Umayyad and Abbasid empires ruling from Damascus and Baghdad, respectively. But there were no early rules about non-Muslims, newly conquered lands, tax collection, minting of coins; nor were there a language of trade, security on the roads, or organized sea trade.

Law Schools and Legal Systems

During the years from 632 to 932, there arose a need to address new conditions within the empires. As early Christianity established church councils, so in early Islam it was necessary to create legal systems, through law schools, to regulate the private lives and public mores of the various Islamic communities. Within Sunni Islam there arose four major law schools; among the Shi'i there were three. The legal systems of the schools were grounded in basic Islamic doctrines, but they differed in their reliance on the Sunna as a basis for daily living. Some of the Sunni systems were "liberal," as they are today in Egypt, the Indian subcontinent, and central Asia. Others were more "conservative" systems, such as those practiced in Saudi Arabia and North Africa, and tended to be "strict" and "fundamentalist."

The Shi'i schools were also divided into liberal and conservative systems of legal thought, although it is more accurate to speak of "orthodox" and "esoteric." The Shi'i practices of Iran, for example, are based on the same Shi'i Islamic concepts as those in Syria, North Yemen, and Lebanon. There are, however, considerable differences in interpretations of Shi'ite practices in these countries.

But there was far more to Islam than political, legal, social, and economic issues. During these first three hundred years of endless legal and theological arguments, there emerged a unique civilization. Built solidly on the foundations of older societies, cultures, and philosophies, the medieval Middle Eastern, Asian, and African Islamic peoples and societies were alive with prosperous trade, vibrant literature and well-stocked libraries, new sciences of astronomy, algebra, and navigation. This medieval period is known as the "golden age" of Islam. But it was also a time of mysticism and Sufism.

Sufism and Scholarship

The "sufi" or "wearer of wool" (from *suf*, "wool") was already present within the seventh-century Islamic world. Known as ascetics, the early Sufis wore coarse woolen garments; they were quite similar to the early Christian monks and hermits who lived in isolation from others in order to pray and fast. In time such holy men and women attracted the attention of the poor and displaced people of the country and cities. They were sought out for their advice, support, and "miracles." Upon their deaths, shrines were erected over their tombs, and pilgrims traveled to these shrines on special days to touch the tombs, hang ribbons and petitions, and pray to receive blessing from the tombs of the holy persons.

The Sufi movement of holy men and women grew, so that in the tenth century it was possible to speak of a body of Sufi literature or theology. The Sufi movement had by then left the desert and begun to form communities of Sufis living, praying, and working together. Offering food and refuge to the poor or troubled, such communities became famous for their leaders, followers, and supporters, and for their rituals of initiation and prayer.

Speaking of divine love, of being "intoxicated" by God, as a doctrine the Sufis had by the tenth century created their own explanations of God and change. Popular among the Sufi thinkers was al-Junayd of Baghdad (d. 910). He spoke of humankind's eternal quest for reunion with God, who had willed the separation of humans and the divine and so compelled humankind to strive to die within themselves in order to be reunited with God.

Islamic Sufi scholars developed in ways similar to their various European religious counterparts; some researchers suggest that Islamic mysticism deeply influenced Spanish and Italian mystics. By the twelfth century, Sufi scholarship and its rationalist legalisms were in great part reconciled in the work of the famous Islamic theologian al-Ghazali (d. 1111).

Medieval Islamic Society:
Cultural Expansion

The growth of Islam was about more than schools of law, disputes over political and religious succession, rationalist legalisms, or Sufi exhilaration. Islam concerned itself with nearly every phase of medieval society, from the rights of peasants, the duties of the prince, and the responsibilities of the merchant to the role of the scholar and, in time, the growth of guild systems. Indeed, the medieval period of Middle Eastern and North African history was a period of an incredible expansion of information about landholding, seed experimentation, long-distance land and sea trade, and artisan industries. The sciences associated with trade, agriculture, and crafts flourished in the courts of Baghdad caliphs and North African petty rulers. Baghdad, Cairo, and Tunis became centers of great universities, much like the medieval Christian universities of Paris and Bologna. Scholars would spend months visiting one of the universities and then travel on to another. During their visits they copied handwritten texts about Islamic law, philosophy, and Sufism, poetic works, accounts of travel, histories of regions, geographical details of road systems, trade, and agricultural products.

The flourishing of literature during the medieval period corresponded directly with the expansion of the Islamic state of Medina into the Islamic empires of the Middle East and North Africa. Scholars sought patrons for financial support, while rulers and the courts eagerly sought the brightest scholars. These court scholars provided the intelligence reports needed for optimal government functioning (geographical accounts, trade statistics, accounts of food production), and they, in turn, were provided with time in which to pursue their specialties.

The prosperity from land and sea trade led to growth in the sciences, geography and astronomy, in particular. By the time the Italian Marco Polo set out in the thirteenth century with his father and uncle to "discover" the eastern trade, Arabic- and Persian-speaking travelers and sailors had already explored much of West Africa, the East African coast, parts of India, southeast Asia, and several of the great ports of China. Such land travel and seafaring by Muslim merchants and scholars resulted in the collection of an enormous volume of information in library accounts and manuscripts. The commerce and industry of the empires and petty states were responsible for scientific innovations in mathematics, botany, zoology, physics, chemistry, and agronomy.

Trade between the empires and states also brought the Islamic people into contact with other literatures, cultures, and languages, such as the rich literature of India, the religions of Africa and Asia, and the languages of the coastal and inland peoples. Stories of Indian origin, such as *Sinbad the Sailor* and *Arabian Nights* (the *Thousand and One Nights*) were told and retold. Buddhism and Hinduism brought with them new ways of viewing human life and mysticism. Familiarity with many new languages rekindled interest in Arabic grammar and syntax.

Reform Movements of the Eighteenth and Nineteenth Centuries

Economic and political changes in Europe during the sixteenth to the eighteenth centuries that led to the Industrial Revolution of the eighteenth and nineteenth centuries found the rulers and scholars of the Middle East, North Africa, and India unprepared. Their complacency, an outgrowth of the riches of their own medieval accomplishments, left them ill equipped for the times. While Europe's global appetite for land, gold, and labor during the sixteenth to eighteenth centuries became ravenous, much of the former "golden age" of Islam tarnished and measurably diminished.

A number of textbooks and specialized studies have spoken of the eighteenth and nineteenth centuries as times of decay and stagnation for Third World peoples. Some reasons typically used to explain the decline of the Middle East and Asia were the failure to improve technology, the fragmentation of societies, "oriental despotism," and Islam. Islamic traditions and leaders bore a great deal of the blame for the sad state of affairs in the larger Islamic empires (Ottoman, Iranian, and Moghul Indian). Other Islamic societies, however, such as in West and North Africa, the Caucasus, and Central Asia, did not seem to stagnate or decay to a great extent.

Invasions by British, French, Austrian, and Russian forces into the Middle East, Asia, and Africa during the eighteenth and nineteenth centuries are well-documented invasions that began commercially and ended militarily. Little is known, however, about the continuous waves of rural uprisings and urban-reform movements under the banner of Islam. At times the eighteenth- and nineteenth-century Islamic reformers led insurrections against the "infidel" and, at other times, imposed purges and reforms against their fellow Muslim believers. In both cases the grass-roots movements of Islamic Sufi communities and rural peoples gained momentum even while the imperial administrations slowly collapsed under indebtedness, foreign loans, and sagging revenues. Between 1725 and the late 1880s a number of peasant and pastoral uprisings occurred; they were struggles for land, water, social justice, and fundamental reform under the banners of Sufi communities, rural and urban believers, and town elders. Indeed, twentieth-century Islamic fundamentalism and Islamic resurgence owe much to the eighteenth- and nineteenth-century reform movements.

A typical empire-reform movement of the period was that of the Wahhabis in central Arabia. Beginning in the 1740s under the leadership of Muhammad ibn Abdul Wahhab (d. 1772), the Wahhabis joined forces with the urban merchant family of Ibn Saud and set out to purge the Ottoman Empire of corruption. The Wahhabis rose again and again throughout the nineteenth century, delivering the message of fundamentalist Islam as the solution to the general disintegration of Ottoman rule. In 1902, led by the Saudi family and wrapped in Wahhabi "purist" practices, the movement regained control of central Arabia, which became a kingdom in 1932. The discovery of oil in 1938 firmly established Saudi control over the kingdom.

MODERN ISLAM AND
ISLAMIC PEOPLES

World War I and its aftermath shocked the people of the Middle East, Asia, and Africa more than had previous events: despite the activism of the nationalists and the Islamic leaders, the Islamic world remained firmly under European control. In response to the continued colonial occupation of Islamic lands following World War I, new groups of fundamentalists and reformers emerged. The Muslim Brothers of Egypt (1928), the Fedayan-i Islam of Iran (1945), and the interwar guerrilla warfare of the Libyan leader Omar al-Mukhtar all signaled a new approach to religious reforms and fundamentalist purges. Most Islamic groups were not politically active; the Islamic groups that drew the attention of observers were a minority of urban-based religious activists intent on armed and violent confrontation.

As noted earlier, the roots of today's Islamic "resurgence" lie in the eighteenth and nineteenth centuries; the early years of the twentieth century serve as a distinct model of activism. The post–World War II fundamentalists and reformers, however, were generally defensive, or non-offensive, in nature, intent primarily on purifying the political and social structures of Islamic societies. But they were joined by a third kind of Islamic activist, the "radical" Muslim, whose radicalization took the form of widespread, often violent, activity within the countryside and cities aimed at far-reaching goals of reform and purification. The resurgence so often spoken about is indeed a continuum from earlier times, but more radical in nature. In this sense, while not the first manifestation of radicalism, the Iranian revolution rapidly became militant on both a national and international scale, involving Muslims in Iran, the Gulf, the Peninsula, and the Fertile Crescent. Lebanon's Muslims and Iraq's Muslims are as deeply affected by the events within the Iranian focal center as are Iranians themselves. Curiously, while building internationalist solidarity upon the religious, historical, and cultural themes so central to all Muslims, Lebanon, Iraq, and Iran also display a high level of nationalist aspirations in the name of Islam.

It is perhaps no accident that the Shi'i with their long history of militant confrontation and religious doctrines of Imamate, Return, Interpretation, and Imitation have gained notoriety. The different Shi'i groups, historically at odds with each other, have coalesced into cooperative activism in the Middle East and Asia. Such cooperation was rare in the past, but shared hardships both within and without each country have created a new basis for political and religious cooperation. The new "ecumenism" which is found within both the Sunni and Shi'i worlds is a response to earlier attempts at reform and more recent attempts at revolution undertaken to solve the problems of poverty, hunger, and corruption so prevalent in the contemporary world, and particularly in the Third World.

The Islamic peoples of the world see themselves as an integral part of the twentieth century, and may not be characterized only by those among them who may be fundamentalists, reformers, or radicals. The modern Muslim, sympathetic to the sufferings of Catholic Central and South America and to the activism of liberation theology sees Islam as the solution—stripped as it is of pretensions and rich in fourteen hundred years of tradition and learning. Convinced of the importance of the Prophet's message, the Islamic communities in Miami and Paris and Cairo and Manila are pressing their leaders for greater access to and reestablishment of their religious beliefs.

Previous efforts along these lines have done little to hold back either colonialism or the emergence of secular nationalism, and there are many Islamic leaders who doubt the appropriateness of further political and public activism, preferring to concentrate on the social, private, and political worlds of their respective societies. Certainly not united on all counts, but deeply disturbed by the agony of their people, the Islamic leaders of today speak about unity and quote the Qur'anic verse, "My servants, the righteous, shall inherit the earth." While not successful in creating a theological and political movement similar to the "reformations" of the Jewish and Christian faiths, Islam, through the challenges of the twentieth century, is on the threshold of a renaissance and, for some, the beginnings of an Islamic "reformation." Therein lies the dynamic explosion of contemporary Islam.

FAITH: THE PILLARS OF ISLAM

It should be clear that the beginnings of Islam and the life of the Prophet Muhammad were deeply rooted in both the specific circumstances of western Arabia and the general overall social conditions in the Fertile Crescent and Arabian Peninsula. From the Old Testament, we know that Judaic traditions spring from the Sinai and the lands of the Fertile Crescent, while the New Testament shows the Palestinian roots of Christian customs. So too the Qur'an is filled with the customs and traditions of pre-Islamic Arabia.

Geographical proximity aside, there are some differences, however, between the earlier religions and Islam. Islam has traditionally opposed the veneration of the *person* of Muhammad and, instead, focuses on the *message* or revelation given to the Prophet. Less person-centered than Christianity, Islamic doctrines and practices have derived either out of pre-Islamic Arabia or from the messages revealed to Muhammad. Muslims are not therefore known as the "people of Muhammad" (or, as is mistakenly stated, "Muhammadans") as

Christians are the people of Christ. In this respect, the prophethood of Muhammad is similar to that of Moses, to whom God's laws also were revealed. In Islam, God's revelations in the Book are the center of Islamic doctrines and practices, and Muslims are therefore the people of the Book.

The Qur'an is the centerpiece of Islam. In addition, the traditions, or narratives (in Arabic, the word is *hadiths*), of the Prophet were handed down from generation to generation as rules of Islamic behavior or practice. In time, the Qur'an and the *hadiths* formed the basis of Islamic law and jurisprudence, philosophy and theology, and doctrines and practices. Understanding the Qur'an and the *hadiths* is fundamental for understanding Islam, as are the Gospels for Christianity and the Talmud for Judaism.

The beliefs and practices of Muslims are separated into the Pillars of Faith and the Pillars of Worship. Neither group by itself is enough. Faith and the implementation of that faith, the worship, must go hand in hand.

The Pillars of Faith

The Pillars of Faith, or doctrines, of Islam are central to the life of believers. They are:

1. God's Oneness
2. The Prophethood of Muhammad
3. The Book or Qur'an
4. The Final Judgment
5. The Existence of Angels and Jinns.

The first pillar of Islam and the most important is the concept of the unity of God. God, and God alone, is worshiped. Supreme creator, lawgiver, provider, judge, and sustainer, God's attributes numbered ninety-nine. In reciting the ninety-nine attributes or names of God, a Muslim recites a "rosary," or prayer beads, in order to remember the all-encompassing nature of the one powerful and transcendent God who is both Merciful and Compassionate.

The Prophethood of Muhammad is the second pillar of Islam. Muhammad is called the "Messenger of God." As God sent Adam and then Noah, Abraham, Moses, David, and Jesus, so God sent Muhammad. In the Qur'an, Moses is called the "Spokesman of God," Abraham the "Friend of God," and Jesus the "Spirit of God" and "Word of God." But Muhammad is the "Messenger" and the final prophet.

The third principal belief of Islamic peoples is the Pillar of the Book or Qur'an. The Qur'an, which was revealed to Muhammad in Arabic, is considered to be the fulfillment of God's messages to humankind. A reading of the Qur'an quickly discloses its Judeo-Christian roots — stories of Mary and the birth of Jesus, David and the prophets of the Old Testament, the Children of Israel, and Adam. For Muslims, then, the people of the world are divided into the people of a Book and the people without a Book. Christians have the New Testament, and the Jews the Old Testament. Traditional Islamic tolerance of Judaism and Christianity as "religious cousins" began with the importance Islam placed on the written account of a religion's message.

Because the Qur'an is the revealed Word of God, it is considered sacrilegious to trace the development of the religious and legal ideas in the Book. It is doubtful that the Qur'an was in written form as one volume, at the time of Muhammad's death in 632. After his death, however, a codex, or manuscript, of the Qur'an was prepared by Abu Bakr, his father-in-law, who was publicly chosen as first caliph, the spiritual and political successor to Prophet Muhammad. The third of the early caliphs, Uthman, commissioned a committee to produce an authoritative text in the original Arabic, which text has ever since been the only version of the Qur'an. Even so, as late as the tenth century, seven variations of the Qur'an were known to exist, discrepancies between them and the original due to mispronunciations of a small number of words in various dialects.

The fourth and fifth pillars of Islam are those of the Final Judgment and of Angels and Jinn. The former is similar to the Christian view of Heaven, Hell, the Day of Judgment, and the Resurrection. As the fifth pillar, the Qur'an mentions that the angels are creatures of God who record humankind's deeds, witness the Day of Judgment, and serve those favored by God. The jinn (*jinni* is the singular) were created by God as spirits; some of them are good spirits, but others rebelled and became "satans." The leader of the "satans" is Iblis, an angel who fell from God's grace when he disobeyed God's command to bow down to Adam. Iblis pridefully refused to humble himself, as an angel, before Adam, the man, whom God had specifically created as God's deputy on earth.

The Pillars of Worship

The Pillars of Worship, that is, the practices of Islam, are the practical and visible side of Islam. The basic Pillars of Worship are five:

1. A profession of faith
2. Daily prayer
3. Annual offerings
4. An annual fast of thirty days
5. A pilgrimage to Mecca.

Two other "pillars" are sometimes considered fundamental to Islam, but not by all. One is holy war or *jihad;* the other is good works. All Muslims, however, adhere to the first five pillars as the basic practices of the believer.

Every Muslim declares in the daily call to prayer, "There is no God but God, and Muhammad is his Messenger." As the First Pillar of Worship, this act serves as both a reminder of submission to the message of Islam and a reaffirmation of the unity of God and the Prophethood of Muhammad. From birth to death this invocation is an integral part of a Muslim's life, whispered into the ear of the new-born child, proclaimed in the thick of battle, and uttered at graveside. The profession of faith is the constant and continuous witness of all Muslims to the fundamental core of Islam.

The second pillar is the recitation of daily prayers at dawn, in early afternoon, mid-afternoon, at sunset, and at night. The prayers are recited in Arabic. The person assumes a series of different postures while facing Mecca. Muslims face Mecca while praying because their holiest shrine, the Ka'ba, with its sacred black stone, has been there since pre-Islamic times. The fixed prayers and praying positions are preceded by a ceremony of purification of different parts of the body. The hands and feet are ritually cleaned, then the face, ears, and eyes, in preparation for the Muslim's communication with Allah.

Islam, like Christianity and Judaism, prefers communal prayer and worship in a place designated specifically for worship: for the Muslim, this is a mosque. At the same time, however, to Muslims the whole earth is a mosque, so they are permitted to worship anywhere, in congregation or alone. Thus, as in Judaism, Islamic practice allows the believer to pray wherever he or she is working or living, such as an open field, a factory, an office, at home, in fact, in any place except a rest room or a cemetery. Led by an *imam*, or prayer leader, the Muslim faithful usually pray together on Friday. While Islam has no sabbath, during Friday's congregational prayer, everyone must stop all activity and go to the mosque.

The third pillar requires Muslims to pay a religious tax every year. Traditionally, this tithe, or *zakah*, ordered every Muslim to pay two and one-half percent of his or her accumulated wealth, either in cash, goods, or produce. The payments were turned over to the principal religious leader in the village or town primarily for general welfare, and for use in the maintenance of hospitals, religious schools, mosques, religious lecture halls, or cultivated lands. The payment of *zakah* has a second purpose: to emphasize that the love of Allah must be greater than the love of riches.

A month of fasting, during which Muslims may swallow nothing, not even water, is the Fourth Pillar of Worship. During Ramadan, the ninth month of the Islamic calendar, complete fasting is demanded from sunrise to sunset, as is sexual abstinence. Ramadan was a month of fasting in the pre-Islamic period and is still considered today to be a time for inner reflection and humility and for strengthening spiritual values.

Evenings are spent with family or friends in breaking the fast. In many instances, one-thirtieth of the Qur'an is read aloud each night in special congregational prayers in the neighborhood mosque. During Ramadan, restaurants are often closed and offices open only in the afternoons.

The fifth pillar is the *hajj*, or pilgrimage. A Muslim who is physically able and can afford to make the usually long and arduous trip is obliged to make at least one pilgrimage to Mecca during her or his lifetime. The pilgrimage is always made during Dhu al-Hijja, the twelfth month of the Islamic year. Since the Muslim calendar is a lunar one, and its year is only 354 or 355 days long, the Muslim year and its holidays and events move forward through a cycle of thirty-three Muslim years before repeating a date. This means, of course, that the dates for both Ramadan and *hajj* move forward year by year and are not seasonal.

The *hajj* is a return to the earliest sources of Islamic beliefs. More than four thousand years ago, Prophet Abraham built the Ka'ba, the house of the one God, in Mecca. The ordeals and afflictions of Abraham and his family were retraced in pre-Islamic worship and were later purified of idolatry and retained in Islam by Prophet Muhammad. Since the time of Prophet Muhammad the Ka'ba has been the holiest sanctuary of Islam.

Every year almost two million Muslim pilgrims reach Mecca by land, air, or sea to take part in the various rites of the *hajj,* which lasts five days. Following much the same pattern as did pre-Islamic pilgrims to Mecca, the Muslim male pilgrim *(hajji)* sheds all distinctive dress and dons seamless two-part white clothing; women may wear their usual sewn clothes. Then the pilgrim proceeds to the Great Mosque and the Ka'ba, walks seven times counterclockwise around the Ka'ba's cubic structure and, if it is possible, kisses the black stone. He or she then drinks the water of the sacred well of Zamzam at the shrine of Prophet Abraham. The pilgrim walks seven times between the mounts Safa and Marwah in commemoration of the trials of Hagar, as she sought aid and water. (Hagar was the handmaiden of Prophet Abraham's wife, Sara, and the mother of Ishmael, Abraham's elder son, the ancestor of the Arabs.) After visiting the plain of Arafat, fifteen miles from Mecca, and stoning the three stations of Satan in Mina, the pilgrim completes the spiritual rites with the sacrifice of a sheep, cow, or camel.

Through the experiences of the pilgrimage, many Muslims gain a sense of solidarity with their faith. The *hajj* is an intensely emotional experience. Participating in that experience with thousands and thousands of peoples of all lands, races, languages, and cultures lets the *hajji* realize and appreciate the extent and potential of the Islamic world.

While commerce, as in pre-Islamic days, still plays a part in the pilgrimage, today political sentiment and activity are becoming increasingly invasive. In 1979 the Great Mosque was seized by Islamic fundamentalists and held for two weeks in protest against the Saudi rulers. And since the Iranian revolution, Iranian pilgrims have engaged in continuous political activities during the pilgrimage.

Some Muslims view holy war or *jihad* as another "pillar" of worship. *Jihad* means "struggle" in the sense of a struggle against ungodliness in oneself or in the community. It also has come to mean a "war" in the sense of the holy wars or crusades of the medieval period in which Muslims defended the Holy Land against the invading enemies of Islam. Viewing the world as divided into lands of Islamic rule and lands of the nonbelievers, the medieval Muslim states of North Africa and the Middle East justified their conflicts with the nonbelievers as the rightful and worthy duty of devout Muslims. Such wars were, in time, even extended to include purges or reform movements within Islamic lands. Indeed, although the Muslim must not begin such wars, the Qur'an states that warfare is necessary:

> Fight in the way of Allah against those who fight against you, but begin not hostilities. Lo! Allah loveth not aggressors.
>
> (Qur'an, 2:190)

or

> And fight them until persecution is no more, and religion is for Allah. But if they desist, then let there be no hostility except against wrongdoers.
>
> (Qur'an, 2:193)

In recent times, the concept of holy war has taken on a different meaning. Today, in the hills of Lebanon or on the plains of Iran or in rain forests of the Philippines, holy war is said to be the just cause of all Muslims against poverty, disease, ignorance, and injustice. The new Islamic "strugglers" have fought against colonial and imperial foes alike in the belief of immediate reward in heaven upon dying in battle. Not all Muslims, however, share such a wide interpretation of the pillars of Islam, although many saw the overthrow of the Shah of Iran or the seizure of the Great Mosque in Mecca as the fulfillment of the sixth "pillar" of worship.

Considered by some Muslims to be yet another "pillar" is the obligation to do good works, behave honestly, and refrain from alcohol, the eating of forbidden meat, and usury. Such observances are expected to ensure entrance into heaven on the Day of Judgment.

HOLIDAYS

Id al-Fitr (Small Festival) and Id al-Adha (Great Festival) are the most important holidays. Id al-Fitr celebrates the breaking of the fast at the end of the ninth month, Ramadan. Celebrated during the first three days of the tenth month, it is the most widely observed holiday. Id al-Fitr is a joyous festival, celebrated by giving to charity, wearing new clothes, visiting family and friends, and feasting on savory foods.

Id al-Adha lasts for four days, from the tenth through the thirteenth of Dhu al-Hijja, the twelfth month of the Muslim calendar. The first day begins with prayer; then, if the family can afford it, a sheep, cow, or camel is sacrificed. This follows the tradition of Prophet Abraham, who attempted to sacrifice his firstborn son, Ishmael, in obedience to God's command (God replaced Ishmael by a ram). The meat of the sacrifice is then divided among the poor, friends and relations, and the family. This tradition remains today exactly as it has always been. The remaining days of the holiday are celebrated in a joyous spirit similar to that of Id al-Fitr.

MISCONCEPTIONS

Misconceptions about Islam chiefly fall into two categories: politics and family and personal life. During the last twenty-five years, increased political and economic unrest in Muslim countries has focused attention on the Islamic world and has created interest in Islam. But, because Islamic life is so different from what the West is familiar with, misconceptions in interpretation and understanding have arisen.

Many Muslims, particularly those whose affinity with their faith is of a more religious nature, believe that the information proffered to non-Muslim countries, which often comes from non-Muslims, is subjective, frequently even misinformed. When their points of view seem to reflect incomplete documentation, personal interpretation, or a distaste for Muslim people, such writers are called "orientalists" by Muslims. Orientalism, accordingly, signifies the reporting of misconceptions and misinformation. The misconceptions are not always intentional; they can arise from biases of any nature. To Muslims, it is important that they be corrected before they lead to or compound misunderstandings and hostilities.

Western historians and members of the media sometimes have little or no knowledge of the Qur'an and consequently cannot understand certain Muslim activities, be they political or religious. Both the politics and religion of Muslim life are parts of a single, all-encompassing, divinely inspired religion embodied in the Qur'an and the Sunna (the way of the Prophet Muhammad). Any divergence from the tenets laid down therein is false to Islam. So, to understand and to report accurately on Islamic matters requires at least some familiarity with the totality of the religion.

Misconceptions may further arise from the Western acceptance of the behavior of those nations or individuals that have veered from the pure faith of Islam for their own various purposes as standard to Islam. An observer of such a "Muslim" nation may see the behavior of the people and the conditions under which they live as reflective of true Islam, when in fact the person is erroneously viewing Islamic society from a secular perspective, forgetting it is a religion that encompasses all of life—a religion that in certain instances is only partially adhered to.

It would be simple to blame misunderstandings and misconceptions entirely on non-Muslim Western writers. But Muslims are, on occasion, misinformed about Islamic doctrine and base their understandings on a range of sources—from the Qur'an through the *hadith, Sunna, Shari'a,* and other interpretations. But these other interpretations, whether they originate with scholars, schools of religious thought, or more secular sources, often differ in their strict adherence to the Qur'an and create their own inconsistencies and misconceptions. Consequently, it is understandable, given misinformation on both sides, that Western writers quite unintentionally offend some more conservatively oriented Muslims.

Particularly in non-Muslim countries like the United States, some of the most common misconceptions about Islam relate to women and the family, divorce, polygamy, and *jihad* and fundamentalism.

The Status of Women in Society and in the Family

The position accorded women by the Qur'an and the *Shari'a* (the code of Islamic law) contrasts markedly with the treatment permitted in pre-Islamic days by a father or a husband and his male relatives. The Qur'an, the *hadiths,* and the *Shari'a* recognize the equality of women and men. As a result of the greater freedom granted to women by Islam, and following the practices instituted by Prophet

Muhammad after the *hijra,* women were able to play a substantive and definitive role in Muslim life and accomplishments.

Nevertheless, since the death of Prophet Muhammad, various scholars and students of the Qur'an have interpreted several passages in ways that seem to deviate from the fundamental concept of the equality of the sexes as originally stated in the Qur'an. For example, one such passage stipulates that men should support women financially and protect them; in return, a woman owes obedience to her husband, even in his absence, and may be punished if disobedient. Although there is much Qur'anic legislation dealing with the relationship between women and men, much of it has been bypassed or discarded in Muslim cultures in order to maintain patriarchal supremacy and male domination. Today, Muslim women in general do not have rights equivalent to Western women.

The preference among Muslim families for male children derives in some part from a concern among families that girls are more vulnerable and need greater protection. It is, further, the hope of Muslim families that their firstborn be a boy so that he can, with his father, be a breadwinner and supporter of the family.

Before the time of Prophet Muhammad, women were accorded little dignity or status; rather, as in many pagan societies, they were considered sexual bait, even property to be bought and sold. The Qur'an corrected that situation by prescribing both modesty and equality of status for women. To secure such modesty, the Qur'an advises that women wear "proper" clothing and refrain from what might be misconstrued as suggestive gestures and glances. From the Qur'an, women learn to find respect for themselves within themselves, not in such things as dressing in a provocative way.

The average Muslim woman in America generally follows the behavior prescribed by the Qur'an, but adapts it to the American lifestyle. She tries to be modest in clothing and actions but, at the same time, the more comfortable life-style dictates less rigidity of conformance to strict Muslim observance regarding dress. Moreover, Muslim women leave their heads uncovered except in the mosque or at prayer. Muslim women may work, although they shun occupations that can lead to much physical contact with men, such as nursing or serving in a restaurant. They take part in political activities and even run for public office.

Approximately five percent of Muslim women in America are quite conservative, their behavior and dress are more strictly limited. Their attire can be extreme, and there are restraints on their conduct that may be compared with those imposed on Hasidic Jewish women. For the most part, though, Muslim women in America are freer and more independent in their devotion to Islam.

All Muslim women do not willingly accept the restrictions placed upon them merely because they have borne them for a long time. Rather, one may expect that they will struggle harder in the future to resume the rights granted by the Qur'an but usurped by male-dominated societies. Political and public activities are areas in which Muslim women have already taken giant steps toward equality or even prominence. Egypt and Iran have seen women marching alongside the men and at times taking their places. The election of Benazir Bhutto to the presidency of Pakistan is an important indication of changes in the perception of women.

Divorce

The Qur'an says that marriage is a union for life. The man and the woman make the choice voluntarily on the basis of religion, morality, devotion, and affection. Unsuccessful marriages may legally be ended by divorce, but divorce is the last option. Islam teaches that divorce is displeasing to God; therefore, according to the *Shari'a,* specific efforts must be made to reconcile the spouses.

Divorce among Muslims in the United States is subject to the civil laws of the various states, just as with people of any other religious faith. A divorce is authoritative, and husband and wife are free to go their separate ways. If a Muslim couple residing in the United States were married in an Islamic state, however, where the contract is not only civil but also a religious contract with God, a divorce is a matter of conscience as well. For complete freedom, particularly in the case of remarriage, a conscientious and religious man will dissolve his marriage by declaring his (and his wife's) freedom before an appropriate Muslim authority. This last action is not too dissimilar to the "get" required by Jewish law to dissolve the marriages of conservative Jews.

Divorce courts do exist in most Islamic states, and there are criteria

by which a judge will allow a divorce: if, for example, staying together will be disruptive to a proper family environment and dam-
aging to the welfare of any children of the union, a divorce may be
granted. A Muslim man is generally ordered to pay his wife the remaining balance on the dowry (or "bridewealth") he promised at the
time of marriage and to reimburse any personal funds or possessions
she brought to the marriage. On occasion he will be ordered to pay
alimony. While custody decisions differ among the schools of law,
custody of children younger than six or seven years of age is generally
given to the mother. Daughters remain with their mothers until puberty or marriage, according to the operative school of law. A boy,
however, is placed in his father's custody at puberty, a legislated age
that can vary from sect to sect and from country to country.

Polygamy (Polygyny)

Sura 4 of the Qur'an restricts to four the number of wives allowed to
a Muslim man. To marry more than one woman, a man should be
wealthy enough to support additional wives, emotionally and financially. A Muslim man may always take an additional wife in certain
situations: if his wife is terminally ill, if she is incapable of childbearing, or if their sexual life is dysfunctional. In any case, the husband is
obligated to treat all his wives equally, and each is granted the same
rights and privileges. Some Muslim scholars believe that it is the right
of a first wife, if she obtained such a commitment from her husband
at their wedding, to insist that he be monogamous.

Another situation in which marriage to more than one woman is
permitted is when the normal numerical ratio of men to women is
skewed by war, disease, or other such calamity. Since the care of wid-
ows and single women is incumbent upon Muslim men, the assump-
tion of multiple wives has been seen as a logical way of affording
marriage to any woman who desires it.

Jihad

The importance of *jihad* cannot be underestimated, but the undue emphasis by Western media on the military and aggressive aspects of the
struggle diminishes its significant moral and spiritual implications.

The term *jihad* is often incorrectly translated as "holy war," a term coined by the West. If the phrase in English were to be translated back into Arabic literally, that Arabic term would not be found in the Qur'an, the *hadiths,* or any other Islamic literature. Unfortunately, the widespread use of the term, combined with a general lack of fluency among most Muslims in both English and Arabic, have led to the acceptance of the term "holy war," even in Muslim societies.

The concept of *jihad* as primarily a "holy war" incorporating terrorist activities is rooted in a lack of familiarity with the concept of theocracy—the religious and political dimensions of Islam. A Muslim is expected to fight against any individual or any state that infringes upon a Muslim's duty, according to the Qur'an, to establish social justice, world peace, and an environment conducive to the exercise of human rights.

As noted earlier, on a more general and personal basis, *jihad* refers to the individual's struggle to better him- or herself and the surrounding world.

A distinction must be made between *jihad* and fundamentalism. The word *fundamentalism* is currently misused. Most Muslims, regardless of their nationality, their type of government, or their geographic location, are proud to be fundamentalists, which simply means that they believe that Islam and only Islam can provide solution to the many injustices, exploitations, and abuses in the world today.

Islamic Fundamentalism

KHALID BIN SAYEED

Islamic society, from the days of the Prophet in the seventh century, has historically represented a total merger of religion and politics. While today Islamic fundamentalism may take one of several forms, the common and central theme animating each of them is the adherence of all of society to certain essential Islamic laws and practices. Islamic fundamentalists advocate the capture of the state in order to pursue their social and economic objectives—the reestablishment of specific Islamic laws imposing Qur'anic penalties for crimes such as

Khalid Bin Sayeed is Professor of Political Studies at Queen's University in Kingston, Canada.

robbery and adultery, and the establishment of an Islamic welfare system through the institution of *zakat* or alms tax. Fundamentalists also agree that banning *riba*, interest on bank loans and deposits, is vital to the Islamic economic system.

Islamic fundamentalists may be divided into two groups—conservatives (or moderates) and radicals (or revolutionaries). The conservatives, or moderates, advocate the establishment of an Islamic society or state through peaceful, persuasive means. The radicals, or revolutionaries, believe in a violent outright seizure of the state. Similarly, the radical reforms that the revolutionaries advocate assign considerable importance to state control of the economy, the goal being a more egalitarian society. And the radicals tend to be more anti-West in their economic and political ideas than are the conservatives or moderates.

All fundamentalists believe that since the eighteenth century Muslims have experienced a steady decline in both their political commitment and their commitment to practicing the basic principles and rituals of Islam. This decline they believe is due to Western domination of Muslim lands. The fundamentalists further argue that those Muslim states that won their independence from Western rule have set up their governments along secular lines; thus they have not established a pure form of Islamic society. Nor were the countries successful in eliminating Western political and cultural influences. Therefore all fundamentalists have advocated waging *jihad* (holy war or struggle). They argue, though, that this struggle is unlike the traditional *jihad*, which is a defensive war waged to protect Islamic territory. The struggle they advocate would be waged not only against the West but against corrupt Muslim regimes as well.

Modern Islamic radical fundamentalism began with the creation of the Muslim Brotherhood in Egypt during the late 1920s. Its objectives were to introduce the Islamic *Shari'a* (Islamic law) and to eliminate foreign or British influence from Egypt. The Muslim Brotherhood's relationships with the state have ranged from partial cooperation with certain regimes, such as President Nasser's, to outright opposition to others. This opposition led to the movement being banned and its leaders imprisoned or killed. Its support came primarily from urban groups, such as labor, university intellectuals, and a small number of military officers. The *ulama* (learned authorities on Islam) have either remained largely uninfluenced or continued to cooperate with the government. This has been a problem in all Sunni countries where the *ulama* tend to be under government control. Thus the fundamentalist movement in Sunni countries has not yet become a mass movement. Another factor that explains fundamentalism's limited appeal in a country like Pakistan is that a fundamentalist movement like the Jamaat-i-Islami has taken conservative positions on matters such as land reform and expansion of state control over industry and trade.

In Shi'ite countries, like Iran, the clerics are either autonomous or defiant toward the state. In Iran, the fundamentalist movement emerged as a revolutionary struggle against the Shah and in 1979 succeeded in replacing his regime with an Islamic regime dominated by the clerics under the leadership of Ayatollah Khomeini. It is important to note that from the beginning the movement was both anti-Shah and anti-West. The fundamentalists denounced the Shah as anti-Islamic and pro-West in his attempts to set up a secular and pro-West regime in Iran.

From the Western point of view, the most disturbing feature of Islamic fundamentalism has been the violence that some of the fundamentalists have preached and practiced. Unfortunately, Western governments have not tried to understand its causes. Islamic fundamentalists view the policies of the West as systematic attempts to establish Western domination over Muslim lands, and the policies toward Israel as insensitive to the demand of the Palestinians for a homeland. Some Islamic fundamentalists have resorted to violence in their attempts to confront Western domination as it is evidenced in the un-Islamic policies of some of the pro-West Muslim rulers. These tactics have not worked, and there is a tendency among even certain hard-core fundamentalist groups toward pragmatism and reconciliation with the dominant powers.

The recent abandonment of violence as a major instrument of action in Egypt by the Muslim Brotherhood and Iran's willingness to agree to a ceasefire in the Iran-Iraq war are indicative of this trend. It is important to note that terrorism and violence are weapons used by people who, in contrast to the power and glory that their religion has promised them, find themselves living in a state of humiliation.

8

WHY I AM
A MUSLIM

JAMES (JIMMY) E. JONES

> Say ye: "We believe
> In God, and the revelation
> Given to us, and to Abraham
> Isma'il, Isaac, Jacob,
> And the Tribes, and that given
> To Moses and Jesus, and that given
> To (all) Prophets from their Lord:
> We make no difference
> Between one and another of them:
> And we bow to God (in Islam)."
> Qur'an 2:136, A. Yusuf Ali ed.

I have chosen to discuss why I am a Muslim by focusing on the English translation of key Arabic words or phrases that inform my life as a believer in the religion of Al-Islam. The Arabic language is important to Muslims for two major reasons. First, it is the language in which God, through the Angel Gabriel, gave the Holy Qur'an to Prophet Muhammad. Second, it unifies the worldwide Islamic community in that a Muslim from any culture can pray with understanding in any other Islamic culture. My intent is to familiarize the reader with the religion of Islam as it affects my daily life and Muslims' relationships with Christians and Jews.

Bismillah!! The English translation of this Arabic phrase, which means "with the name of God," is the most appropriate place for me

James E. Jones is the Islamic Services Chaplain at the Community Correctional Center in New Haven, Connecticut. He is also on the staff of the APT Foundation, a substance-abuse service agency in New Haven.

to begin describing why I am a Muslim. In a world of people over-whelmed by their self-importance, this phrase brings me proper perspective. As an Afro-American growing up in the South, I learned to appreciate the power and glory of God through my intense participation in the Baptist church. I sang in choirs, performed in church plays, read Scriptures during services, and went to and ultimately taught Sunday school. By the time I left home for college, being Christian was an integral part of my being. Thus, while I was an undergraduate at Hampton Institute in Virginia, I was a member of the campus Chapel Board. A Southern Baptist Christian, my belief in what Muslims call the divine ordinance of God was fundamental to my understanding of the world. So in many ways my intense youthful sojourn in the church prepared me for acceptance of the Islamic idea that absolutely all power comes from God. Consequently, it was very easy for me to understand that the Muslim should begin every act with *Bismillah*, "with the name of God."

Allah-u-Akbar!! The English translation of this Arabic phrase, "God is the Greater," helps to explain my conversion to the religion of Al-Islam. While my experience as a Christian taught me to love and believe in the ultimate power of God, something was missing for me. In particular, I was bothered by my sense that many Christians appear to take their religion seriously only when they are in church, ignoring many of its teachings in their everyday lives. Christianity, as I understood it, did not seem to give enough clear guidance for everyday living. Al-Islam, on the other hand, reflected its consistent emphasis on the ultimate supremacy of God by providing a clear, structured framework for striving to carry out that belief in daily living.

I have found, for example, the systematic prayer at required times in the course of each day to be a spiritual anchor in a turbulent, transitory world. Almost every movement of this mentally and physically exacting worship of God is punctuated by the phrase *Allah-u-Akbar,* (God is the Greater). As a college administrator with a private office, it is easier for me to pray on time than it is for many other Muslims who work in non-Islamic settings where they have no privacy. Additionally, because of lack of knowledge and misinformation among non-Muslims about the Islamic faith, Muslims often face hostility at any overt attempt to practice our faith. As Muslims, we are required

to (1) consistently bear witness that there is no God but the One God;
(2) pray at least five times daily at stated times; (3) give to charity;
(4) fast at least during the lunar month of Ramadan; and (5) go on
pilgrimage to Mecca, if we can afford to do so. In doing these things
the Muslim consistently confirms the idea of *Allah-u-Akbar.*

Al-Salaam-Alaikum!!   Most Muslims use this phrase to greet each
other, as do those American-born Muslims I know. The English translation, "Peace be Unto You," indicates one reason I have stayed in Al-
Islam since my official conversion in October 1979. The phrase signifies the fact that Al-Islam is ultimately a religion of peace: in striving
to submit our wills to God and God's law, we are trying to come into
harmony with, rather than struggle against, creation. This greeting of
peace is the best that one can wish for another person. For me, such
a greeting is also part of the cement bonding our community together,
not only with each other, but with others in the world who seek
peace under God's will. Thus, when both Muslims and non-Muslims
give this or a similar greeting, we enthusiastically return it with *Wa-
Alaikum-Asalaam,* which means "And unto you be peace." The atti-
tude reflected in these greetings is consistent with our articles of faith,
which are: (1) the acknowledgment that there is no God but the One
God; (2) belief in all the Scriptures of God; (3) acceptance of all the
prophets of God; (4) belief in angels; (5) belief in the Day of Judgment and life after death; (6) belief in the divine ordinance. Also
called *Qadr* or Destiny, the divine ordinance tells us that nothing occurs except by the authority of God and with accountability to God.
This does not mean predestination, however; a person still has the
right of choice but must live through eternity by the consequences of
that choice.

   Muslims strive for peace within ourselves, with other people, and
with other groups. The one-dimensional portrayal of our community
as militant is based upon much misunderstanding and gross distor-
tion of motives. It is true, though, that Muslims do not accept peace
at any price. "Peace" for us must include, in addition to justice and
charity, religious freedom for ourselves and for other groups. However, our wish to the world is *Al-Salaam-Alaikum.*

La-iliaha-ill-Allah, Muhammad-un-rasul-Allah!!   The English translation, "There is no God except Allah and Muhammad is his Messen-

ger," is the *Kalimah*, or declaration of faith, that makes me proud to be a Muslim. I am proud because here we aggressively assert the idea of one God, a single God, to the exclusion of multiple personifications of the divine.

As a monotheistic religion, Islam traces its roots back through such Prophets as Abraham, Ishmael, Isaac, Jacob, Moses, and Jesus. Thus, the God we refer to as Allah is the same God that these prophets worshiped. We believe that those who correctly follow the religion of these prophets will also receive their reward in the Hereafter. This is why I, as a Muslim, feel strong kinship with people who are Jews or Christians. Despite differences in theology and religious practices, we have much in common.

The second part of this *Kalimah*—"Muhammad is his Messenger"—provides the greatest challenge in terms of trying to get non-Muslims to understand our religion. Because we mention Prophet Muhammad's name in close proximity to God's, some people mistakenly believe that we worship a prophet (thus the misnomer Muhammadans). For me, a practicing Muslim, this proximity has had the opposite effect. First, it is clear to me that the power and authority of one who does the sending is greater than that of one who is sent, so the phrase reinforces the monotheistic bent of the first part of the *Kalimah*. Second, this phrase reinforces our belief that, while we should make no distinction among God's prophets, Muhammad is the "seal," the last of the prophets: no others will follow him. Additionally, since we can never totally comprehend the Creator, Muhammad is a blessing from God in that he, like other prophets, was sent to warn and to be a role model. We have here, then, a clear, balanced message: on the one hand we are to try to emulate Muhammad; on the other, he is clearly and simply a flesh-and-blood messenger of Allah in the tradition of prophets before him.

Given the overall power and richness of this statement, it is small wonder that all Muslims enter the body of Al-Islam by publicly stating some form of *La-iliaha-ill-Allah, Muhammad-un-rasul-Allah.*

Al-hamdu lillah!! This means "All praise is due to God." In daily life, I strive to live this ideal. In a society where greed, selfishness, and pride are often looked upon as useful attributes, it is difficult to keep a proper perspective. What sustains me is the knowledge that, in spite of tremendous difficulties in my life, God has blessed me by allowing me to find and come into this beautiful religion. The reality of this blessing is highlighted by the fact that racism has no place in Al-Islam. Our religion makes no distinctions based upon race, color, or culture. We are all members of one humanity and one creation under the authority of the One God worshiped by the likes of Abraham, Moses, and Jesus.

As a newly aware young Afro-American college student in 1966, I began, after reading the *Autobiography of Malcolm X*, an aggressive search for an identity that would somehow bring personal and political liberation for me and my people. In the process I found a religion and a way of life that strengthens my feeble human attempts to fight evil and injustice. It is clear to me that Islam's concepts of one God, one creation, and one humanity are and will always be major weapons in fighting against the ills that affect individuals and all of humanity.

Bismillah **(with the name of God) reminds me that the authority for every action comes from God.** *Allah-u-Akbar* (God is the Greater) reinforces the idea that no one or thing is equal to God. *Al-Salaam-Alaikum* (Peace be Unto You) keeps me aware of the peace one attains in striving to serve God. Through *La-iliaha-ill-Allah, Muhammad-un-rasul-Allah* (There is no God except Allah and Muhammad is his Messenger), I focus on the need to publicly declare my allegiance to God and my acceptance of God's messengers. From my perspective as a Muslim, I believe that people make far too much of our "differences." This has been tragically so with religion as we witness past and current wars based upon religious discord. The "children of Abraham" (Jews, Christians, and Muslims) have waged some of history's bloodiest and most unjustifiable wars in the name of God. I pray that we will come to our senses and seek an even greater understanding of the commonality that for most of us already exists. If we can accomplish this, *Al-hamdu lillah!*—All praise is due to God!

9

MONOTHEISM: A CODA

It is overwhelming to think of the number of people who have in common the uncommon legacy of Moses, the "inventor" of monotheism. As we accept the story of and experience the mystery of one God, we move into the awesome stream of Jewish, Christian, and Muslim history, into a body that comprises half the people of the world. It is also overwhelming, then, to look at polls and surveys and see that, with little statistical change over the last fifty years, some 95 percent of the people in the United States claim belief in one God— or at least in a universal spirit.

WHAT WE SHARE

1. We are all people of God. We believe in and are comforted by a transcendent God who is imminent but unknowable. We are "in community" with One not seen, in a family of relationships not limited by time and place. We believe we find God as an active, real presence where we live and work—in the universe, in history.

2. We are all peoples of the Book. We share texts, though not always mutually. The Jews have the Hebrew Bible (i.e., the Christian Old Testament), its first five books called the Torah. Christians have both the Old and the New Testaments with some variations among

---

Lois J. Anderson is the manager of programs and promotions and of volunteer activities at the American Bible Society. She previously served as Director of Communications at Religion in American Life (RIAL), an organization promoting interreligious cooperation through educational research services and public service advertising, provided to all religious communities. She has been a radio, television, and film consultant on the topic of religion and the media.

denominations. For Muslims, the Qur'an speaks of characters from the Bible: Moses, spokesman for God; Abraham, friend of God; Jesus, Spirit/Word of God; Joseph, Aaron, Mary, and others.

3ʹ. We share beliefs in how we ought to live. To integrate those religious beliefs into our way of living, we advocate patterns of ethical behavior and good deeds, thus giving a grounding and direction to our existence.

The Ten Commandments, so often considered negative, are, in truth, quite the opposite. We must live together in mutual respect, measuring our behavior by what God expects rather than by what others expect or demand—or do not. The Commandments tell us how we should be doing something, how we ought to treat God and each other. With this in mind, I share the "Great Commandment" of Jesus: "This is my Commandment that you love one another as I have loved you" (John 13:34). Muslims, too, in their acceptance of the Bible and with the further revelations of the Qur'an, have adopted these beliefs.

4. We share need for "community," which we find in nurturing congregations and in loving homes and nurturing families. We find it in blessings and benedictions, in metaphor and symbol, at communal meals, whether they are ordinary church suppers or extraordinary tables—the Seder, the Lord's Supper, or 'Id al-Fitr. Muslims, Jews, and Christians all work at maintaining group solidarity in order to keep concern for one another's well-being always in mind.

5. Each religion requires certain nonnegotiable practices, observances, or disciplines. Group or corporate worship is a required *action* that calls for physical presence, personal association, and concentration. It speaks to an interdependence among the faithful in order to *be* faithful. Individual daily prayer, as part of life, should be performed by the monotheist. It is a necessary *reaction* to one's knowing that God *is* and that God is at work in life and living.

6. We share a sense of ongoing time and history. This time is not cyclical, as it is in religions concerned with reincarnation. In the search for a universe that has structural unity, time lends importance of a special nature to births, initiations, membership rites, marriages, and deaths. Time is part of planning for development and for the education of children. The monotheist's time continues beyond death, even to some kind of paradise. But with the belief in an after-

life, each religion raises questions about the nature of the afterlife: For whom will it exist? Where will it be? When will we reach it?

7. We expect all believers to give money and time willingly and not as an afterthought. We contribute a share of earnings or wealth, talent and energy, through charity and good work, through education and instruction. These are creative antidotes to selfishness and greed, and are practical demonstrations of priorities, stewardship, and partnership with God.

8. While varying greatly in practice, each religion acknowledges that food has spiritual meaning and power. Diet is often an aspect of religious expression. Spiritual well-being can depend on the physical intake of food and drink. Fasting and feasting have their places. Appreciation of food and its power is enhanced by our various religious persuasions. How many thoughts, how many prayers are in a piece of bread?

HOW WE DIFFER

1. The range of difference in our structures and organizations is wide and varied. Approaches to internal order or harmony extend from the egalitarian, freewheeling, and democratic, to the highly prescribed and hierarchical. Systems range from the simple to complex bureaucracies and from small regional groups to worldwide organizations.

The Jewish community, for example, has a clear system, or way, of life and obligation, but has no centralized ecclesiastical government. Its leadership consists of the individual rabbi in each congregation. It is a community that formalizes interpretations of lifestyle through history from Orthodox to the more recent Reform, to Conservative and Reconstructionist groupings.

The greatest structural variety is found within Christianity, which contains the traditionally called, ordained, and supervised male and female clergy; mere licensed preachers; commonly acknowledged learned leaders; as well as televangelists.

The locally autonomous, flexible Protestant and other Christian congregational groups generally function with clergy. Many others, however, depend on strong lay leadership, without clergy. Some have clear levels of organization and affiliation, while others have only voluntary associations—regional, national, and international. In this latter group are the "mainline" evangelicals, the neo-evangelicals, the fundamentalists, and the charismatic pentecostalists.

Then there are those Christian bodies with legislative authority for the discipline of their adherents or members. The most impressive and obvious organic unity is found within the Episcopal, Eastern (Orthodox), and Roman Catholic churches. The structure of various religious bodies is demonstrated in their names: "Episcopal," for example, indicates supreme authority in a *body,* the "episcopate" of bishops, not in one person such as the pope; "Presbyterian" signifies a chain of authority invested in elders or presbyters.

Other nonstructural differences in the ways in which religions are organized are demonstrated by names that have acquired religious meaning: (1) Geography—Roman Catholic, Eastern Orthodox, Southern Baptist; (2) Leaders—Lutherans, after Martin Luther; and Mennonites, after Menno Simons; (3) Beliefs—Adventist, Baptist, Pentecostal.

Islam has no organized hierarchy. Yet, while Islam may be nonauthoritarian and egalitarian, it is not democratic. There are Muhammad's successors-by-consensus (caliphs); the prayer leaders, or imams, are the most learned in a congregation. The teachers of the law, or mullahs, and the schools of law exist to apply the rules embodied in the Qur'an through case law. Change or modification is brought about through councils of scholars and religious leaders. Islamic schools of thought and action suggest these words: traditionalists (conservative, fundamentalist, orthodox), modernist (liberal), secularist (esoteric).

2. Our places of worship and our rituals and forms of celebration vary. We worship in sacred, hushed-and-holy sanctuaries, where we move in special, sometimes self-conscious and segregated ways. There are also functional and multipurpose meeting rooms that serve as both a place to worship and a place of assembly for worldly activities.

Architecture varies through symbolism, history, and function. Judaism, Christianity, and Islam all use stained glass windows. Light may come from the sun through clear panes or through the stained glass. The colored glass may be lit from within a building at night to let the world see the stories the windows show, silent witness to the faith and the meaning of the building.

Some places of worship are a feast for the eye. In others there is a deliberate holy emptiness which prompts looking inward. A central pulpit with a Bible on it is witness to an emphasis on the message and on simplicity. A divided chancel with an altar speaks of a more complex approach. Flowers, greens, candles—symbols of hope, liturgical hangings, the colors changing with religious seasons—all are more than decoration. Most mosques are handsomely decorated but sparsely furnished. Prayer is directed toward Mecca, indicated by the niche in the wall called the mihrab. But whatever the style of architecture and decoration, it serves to educate.

We differ in language used. Christian diversity has surely been increased by and developed by missionaries who translated scriptures into the vernaculars of people all over the world—from Aramaic to Greek, Latin, English, and thousands of other languages and dialects. Hebrew and Arabic, of course, are the mandatory languages of Jewish and Islamic texts. Both the sacred Arabic, also a Semitic tongue, and Hebrew, the language of Judaism, are handed down from generation to generation. While Islam is also a missionary religion, its Scriptures are not translated.

Though music is not an element in all worship, it is essential to many. Music may be an offering or an accompaniment, but is never a theatrical performance. It may range from classical to religious pop-sentimental. What is important is that listeners and musicians celebrate a religious experience in a communal ceremony. The soul of an inspired cantor speaks of God to a Sabbath congregation. A worshiper can be touched by the piercing sweetness of trained boy–soprano voices. The response to the ringing overtones of a good choir and organ is spiritual and physical. The vigor of urban gospel music can stir the blood of the most phlegmatic person, as can the zeal of untrained volunteers' voices.

Certain religious-service music can be emotionally threatening. Other music, the regular rhythms of music at a funeral or memorial service, for instance, may comfort and assist in controlling the emotions, thereby offering catharsis and release.

Various styles of dress speak visibly to differences in roles and status. Vestments offer clues to clerical rank. Clothing supplies ceremonial drama in many religious settings, to the extent that, in instances, the term "costume" may be fitting. Yet the robes preachers or rabbis wear have simpler meanings, indicating academic achievement or just the desire for some special dignity. Various religious leaders wear no clerical attire whatsoever; this particularly applies to the Muslim imam.

Clothing generally, however, gives identity and permits recognition, necessary as well as useful, for many clergy or religious, and for religious workers. The clerical collar, for example, until recently has served as visual shorthand, as did a nun's habit. The distinct roles of Muslim men and women can be reflected in the way women in particular sometimes dress with only eyes, hands, and feet visible. Amish dress and simplicity are distinctive, as is the black-hatted, frock-coated attire of Hasidic Jewish men and boys.

3. Practices and discipline requirements vary. Membership gives a person a special identity and various responsibilities that, if met and fulfilled, lead to spiritual growth and maturity. Membership requirements differ among the faiths. In some instances, a person is a member at birth. Without much further nurture or continuing religious education, many such persons remain cultural Christians, cultural Jews. Whatever the faith, a devout member or convert becomes part of that people, taking on the privileges and duties of that faith: decision and commitment are musts. All of these extend from the home to the meeting place to the community. Study is followed by ceremonies—of confirmation, of public declaration and recognition. By contrast, to become a Muslim a person must know, believe, and practice the principles of the faith, and announce the acceptance of Islam before two other Muslims.

Regular attendance at worship, ceremonies, or other functions of the religious community mutually benefits the member and builds stability and dependability for the community. But different kinds of services—from daily observance to weekly worship and special celebration—follow different practices.

Though we share the need for designated times and days to complete our rituals of attendance and prayers, we observe them differently. The Muslim must attend worship on Friday. Sabbath for Jews—the seventh and last day of the Jewish week—begins at sundown on Friday, extending to sundown on Saturday. Some Protestant groups also observe Saturday as the Sabbath, but the great majority of Protestants observe it on Sunday. Roman Catholics observe Sunday as the Sabbath.

Worship may certainly be a solitary experience, but group worship, a gathering of believers, is worship's true significance. The search for God may be composed and elegant. The service may be silent and unadorned, as with the Quakers, the Society of Friends. It may be staid, formal, yet simple. The preaching may be flamboyant and ecstatic, even chaotic or high-powered evangelical. Extempore speaking to concerns, spontaneous testimonies, or responsive *amens* are almost ritual parts of some services. The search for reconciliation with God may require shouting and weeping. Whatever the style, it nurtures the spirit of the individual and community—or should—whether it be daily, on a Sabbath, or during holidays or holy days.

Text reading among faiths and denominations may be designated or freely chosen, always, however, serving to give focus to the thoughts and mutual aims of worshipers.

Religious education encompasses knowledge of texts and history as well as ethical and moral values. Among Muslims, self-instruction is widely practiced. For Jews and Christians instruction may be given by parents, clergy, teachers—in structured schools, even around a dinner table.

Prayer is our reaction to, acknowledgment of, and resonance with the One God. But we differ markedly in our timing, frequency, and methods of prayer, from supplication to thanks, whether memorized or spontaneously offered.

As creatures of the One God, service is our responsibility to and for one another. This responsibility finds expression in both the religious and the secular communities. We all must serve. Our service is generally voluntary, a religious reaction to our faith in God, and voluntary *giving* has become a part of it. Even our givings, or offerings, differ in type and manner, depending on the discipline and group. But a general example among religious groups today is providing meals and shelter to the homeless.

LIVING WITH THE DIFFERENCES

As monotheists there is much we share. But we are also shaped by our personal religious heritages. Religion needs the challenge that comes from thinking through our religious faiths and practices. Experiencing religion is an emotional pilgrimage that demands unrepressed confidence in our own God-given instincts.

But through personal experience we learn what and why others believe what they do. This personal experience adds dimension to the vicarious experiences available through books, television, and newspapers. There are many interfaith groups, but it often takes courage to visit the houses of worship of religious groups other than our own. But it is the ritual, the worship and the seasonal observance that differ from what we know, that we need to see, appreciate, and participate in as fully as nonmembers or nonadherents may.

Most of us share the fundamentals: One God, certain texts, group commitment. But what about the religiously cocooned, the denominationally insulated, the uninformed? Confidence in individual belief can be bolstered by greater knowledge and awareness of the experience and beliefs of others. How can that be encouraged?

The United States Constitution guarantees freedom of religion, putting the responsibility on each of us to choose our own faith. The Constitution also guarantees the principle of separation of church and state, thus ensuring that people of various religious traditions and backgrounds can exist and live together in peace. For most of the world this is a new idea, even though it is two hundred years old. How can we improve the quality and nature of our pluralism?

The media generally limit their reports on religion to news of seasonal observances, events involving a religious authority, or religious scandal. Frequently media professionals consider faith and religion as personal and private and are not comfortable or knowledgable reporting it.

Stereotypes prevail often. The profound experiences of World War II, the ecumenical movement, and Vatican II brought changes. But currently, in the Middle East and parts of Europe, political and economic conflicts involve Christians, Muslims, and Jews. Finding our way across such a landscape is pilgrimage indeed.

Most communities list religious organizations, churches, and synagogues in their classified telephone directories. Mosques are more difficult to locate, but can be found by checking the telephone listing under "Muslim" and "Islamic" for likely entities from which to inquire. Check your newspapers to see what they print, editorially and in their advertising, about religion where you live.

What is the religious history of your faith community? Of your town or city? Where is it written or recorded? Who keeps it? Public libraries, religious libraries, and sometimes museums have combinations of objects and activities that illustrate aspects of religion.

Talk. Discuss possibilities of study and sharing the experience of appropriate religious observances, notwithstanding the different faith line. Work with your own and with other religious leaders in your community for improved communication. Think how to invite others in; think how to get yourselves invited out.

Even among monotheists, paths to the belief in the One God differ. So do styles of arriving at our belief. We may also differ on secular issues, but we must be steadfast in our convictions that true religion embraces all of us. We must resolve that unless we appreciate each other's beliefs humanity will suffer spiritual holocaust. As succinctly expressed by Pierre Teilhard de Chardin, French priest, philosopher, and paleontologist: "We are one, after all, you and I; together we suffer, together exist, and forever will we recreate each other."

Although faithfulness in attendance at your own place of worship is devoutly to be encouraged, the calculated planned visit, or even the spur-of-the-moment kind, to another faith's service or celebration ought only to add to the appreciation of your own.

Keep an open mind. Always ask questions. Ask Why? And Why? again. Perhaps the second Why? will be the most helpful.

GLOSSARY

Note: Terms defined here are those not outlined in the text. Please consult the index for further help.

ADONAI: a variant Hebrew name for God.

APOSTLES' CREED: a Christian creed generally similar to the Nicene Creed, but developed from the confession and baptismal invocation of the apostle Peter.

CANON LAW: the laws of doctrine or discipline as established by ecclesiastical authorities.

B.C.E.: Before the Common Era. Also Before the Christian Era.

C.E.: Common Era, used in place of A.D. Also Christian Era.

CIRCUMCISION: surgical removal of the foreskin of the penis.

COMMUNION, Holy Communion, the Lord's Supper: another term for the Eucharist. First Communion generally takes place at seven or eight. A child receives special instruction in preparation for this sacrament.

CRUSADES: a series of wars waged by medieval Christian armies against the Muslims, at that time called Saracens, to regain the Holy Land.

DIETARY LAWS: rules, differing widely from one faith to another, concerning foods that may or may not be eaten; the how, why, and when of serving foods.

ECUMENICAL MOVEMENT, ECUMENICISM: an effort originally promoting Christian unity and cooperation among churches; now spreading worldwide among all faiths.

ELOHIM: a variant Hebrew name for God.

EVANGELICAL (n.): member of one of various largely conservative

Protestant churches emphasizing salvation by faith and grace, the atoning death of Jesus, and the authority of the Gospels as the fundamentals of Christianity.

EXODUS: the escape of the Jews, who were led by Moses, from bondage in Egypt to the land of Canaan. The title of the second book of the Old Testament, which describes those events.

FERTILE CRESCENT: the belt of green and fruitful lands surrounding the eastern end of the Mediterranean Sea and comprising much of the Middle East.

HAGAR (Hager): mother of Ishmael, eldest son of Abraham; Ishmael is considered an ancestor of Prophet Muhammad.

HASIDIM: Jews of a movement noted for the strictest religious observance and great zeal.

HOLY SPIRIT: the third person of the Christian Trinity.

HOST: the consecrated wafers, or bread, used in the Eucharist.

INQUISITION: a special Roman Catholic tribunal established in the thirteenth century to combat heresy; most notorious in fifteenth-century Spain.

KA'BA: sacred cubic building in Mecca, in which is embedded the sacred black stone.

LOURDES: a town in southwest France where the Virgin Mary appeared to a peasant girl, Bernadette, revealing the miraculous curative powers of a spring. A Roman Catholic shrine exists at the site.

MAGI: the three Wise Men of the East who came bearing gifts for the infant Jesus.

"MARY'S SONG": a liturgical song of praise by the Virgin Mary (Luke 1:46–55). Known as the "Magnificat" when set to music for church services.

MESOPOTAMIAN VALLEY: the formerly green and fertile area between and around the Tigris and Euphrates rivers in what is now Iraq.

NICENE CREED: a detailed doctrine formulated at the Council of Nicaea in 325 C.E., based on an ancient formula of the Christian faith that defines the orthodox doctrine of the Trinity.

PENTECOSTALIST: member of any Christian religious body that stresses revivalism to attain holiness and achieve regeneration, often seeking the "gift of tongues" (incomprehensible speech).

POGROM: the planned, organized destruction of peoples, most frequently Jews in Eastern Europe.

POLYGAMY (Polygyny): the practice of having multiple spouses of either sex, but generally wives. Polygyny pertains specifically to multiple wives.

QUR'AN (Koran): the sacred Book of Islam, containing the revelations of God to Prophet Muhammad.

SABBATH: the day of rest (the seventh day of the week) and worship observed on Saturday (Friday evening through Saturday evening) by Jews, and all day Sunday by Christians. Islam observes no Sabbath, but Friday is its day for mandatory congregational prayer in a mosque.

SHI'ITE MUSLIM: a member of the smaller Islamic sect which believes that Ali, Muhammad's son-in-law, was rightful successor of Muhammad as caliph.

STATIONS OF SATAN: three stone pillars, representing evils of Satan, against which pebbles are thrown symbolically during the Muslim *hajj*.

SUNNI MUSLIM: a member of the majority sect of Islam that believes in popular determination of the caliphs (Muhammad's successors as leaders of Islam).

SURA: one of the 114 chapters of the Qur'an, which are arranged in order of length beginning with the longest.

WAILING WALL: gathering place for Orthodox Jews lamenting the fall of the Jewish nation, near the site of biblical Temple of Solomon, now the Mosque of Omar.

WILLIAMS, ROGER: English-born colonial American clergyman; driven by the Puritans from Massachusetts because his views were too liberal, he founded Rhode Island colony where he established religious tolerance and democratic government.

YARMULKE: the head covering worn by Orthodox Jews at all times, by Conservative Jews at Prayer, and by Reform Jews at will.

INDEX